Truth in Love
Titus Brandsma
CARMELITE

Fernando Millán Romeral, O. Carm.

CARMELITE MEDIA

Voice of Carmel Series, 1

Published by Carmelite Media
© Carmelite Media 2022
2nd Edition 2025

1317 Frontage Road
Darien, Illinois 60561 USA

Phone +1-630-971-0724
Email: publications@carmelnet.org
Website: carmelites.info/publications

Printed Book ISBN: 978-1-936742-29-5
Ebook ISBN: 978-1- 936742-30-1

First published in Spanish as *Titus Brandsma, Carmelite.* Also published in Italian as *Il coraggio della verità* by Àncora Editrice, as *Postavil se zlu* in Czech, and as *Tito Brandsma* in Portuguese.

Layout and Cover design by William J. Harry, O. Carm.

TABLE OF CONTENTS

INTRODUCTION

On November 3, 1985, in St. Peter's Basilica in Rome, Pope John Paul II beatified the Dutch Carmelite, Fr. Titus Brandsma, who had died 43 years earlier in the infamous concentration camp at Dachau, Germany. The decisive testimony in the beatification process was that of the nurse who administered the injection of carbolic acid that ended his life. Fearing possible reprisals, she testified under the false name, Tizia. In his homily, the Pope recalled how Saint Titus had preached and proclaimed a culture of love and forgiveness in the face of the philosophy of Nazism which out of contempt and hatred for humanity reached its culmination in the concentration camps.

Father Titus Brandsma was a multifaceted figure: a very active man, culturally restless, somewhat eclectic, conciliatory in difficult situations, but very firm in his convictions. He was deeply immersed in the world of his day (in media, teaching, and political commitment) with, at the same time, an intense interior life. He was a Carmelite priest, journalist, and professor of philosophy and the history of mysticism at the Catholic University of Nijmegen. Titus became rector of that University in 1932. He was involved in ecumenical dialogue. Entrusted by the Church with important responsibilities, Fr. Titus acted as a representative of the Dutch bishops in several decisive missions, including one which would result in his arrest. A long list of activities, responsibilities, and concerns make his biography of one of the most exciting of the 20th century. Throughout it all, Fr.

Titus remained a man of prayer whose spiritual life would come to the fore, particularly in the crucial moments of his imprisonment. Some scholars of his life and spirituality have not hesitated in considering him to be a true mystic.

For Catholic journalists Fr. Titus became a model of the journalist's vocation, of ethical conviction, and of commitment to the truth. For this reason, in 1988, the International Catholic Union of Journalists (UCIP) created the Titus Brandsma Award, presented every three years to journalists or organizations which excel in their commitment to the value of seeking truth. For Carmelites, Fr. Titus becomes a new shoot of holiness in the already eight-hundred-year-old tree of Carmel. This is why groups, new initiatives, projects, and institutes of spirituality bearing his name have sprung up everywhere. For those of us interested in Judeo-Christian dialogue, he is one of those "Just" who (officially recognized or not yet) could recognize injustice and irrationality and act accordingly. For students of spirituality and mysticism, Fr. Titus was a great popularizer of Dutch spiritual writing, of Rheno-Flemish spirituality, and the works of Saint Teresa of Ávila, whom he deeply admired, all in the language and within the academic culture of the Netherlands. For all of these reasons, the prestigious Institute of Spirituality, incorporated into the Catholic University of Nijmegen, today bears his name.

Finally, for the Dutch people, Titus Brandsma is a national hero, recognized for his brave opposition to the invading Nazi regime, for which he paid with his life. For this reason, he was named the most important Dutch Catholic of the century and the most important citizen of the City of Nijmegen, dedicating to him a museum, streets, squares, and even trains—trains so different from those that crossed the face of Europe, loaded with human beings marked for extermination in one of the worst periods of European and world history. In one of those trains, Professor Brandsma was brought to Dachau through the beautiful Bavarian countryside. It was at Dachau that he would give his life on July 26, 1942.

In 2009 the *Colección Sinergia* of the Emmanuel Mounier Foundation in Madrid, Spain offered me the chance of preparing a brief biography of our Carmelite brother. In a series of snippets and broad brushstrokes, eliminating the critical structure and footnotes of an academic work, we presented his fascinating life. We wanted to introduce the reader to the life and thinking of this witness to the faith in the turbulent twentieth century. That book was translated into Italian (*Il coraggio della verità*, published by Àncora Editrice) and into Czech (*Postavil se zlu*, published by Karmelitánské Nakladatelsví). It is an honor and a real joy for me to be able to present it now to the English-speaking public thanks to Carmelite Media, the publishing house of the Carmelite Province of the Most Pure Heart of Mary. This is an enriched translation with various additions to the original version.1 I am grateful to Fr. William J. Harry, O. Carm., for his interest and efforts in the publication of this book. I also want to thank Br. Tom Murphy, O. Carm., and Fr. Jorge Monterroso Mcrida, O. Carm., both of the PCM Province, and Fr. Simon Nolan, O. Carm., of the Irish Province for their help in making the translation as accurate as possible. I hope that it will help to spread the witness and example of Saint Titus in the United States of America and in other English-speaking countries.

---

1. I include at the end of this book a bibliography in English for those who want to go deeper into some of the aspects of Brandsma's life that we only touch on in this short biography.

Fr. Titus Brandsma in 1940 at age 59. The Second World War was underway and the Netherlands was occupied by the Nazis in May. Fr. Titus was fighting persistent health issues and was exhausted. He spent April in a clinic in Amsterdam.

I

CHILDHOOD, RELIGIOUS VOCATION, AND RELIGIOUS FORMATION

1.1 In Friesland

Anno Sjoerd Brandsma was born on February 23, 1881 at Ugokloster, a small farm near the town of Bolsward, in Friesland, which is the northernmost region of the Netherlands. Titus Brandsma would always maintain a love for the Friesian language and culture, promoting various activities and institutions connected with the Friesian region. Although Friesland has a majority Protestant population, Bolsward has always been a city with a significant Catholic population, with many religious vocations originating there. In the time of Fr. Titus, Catholics accounted for 40% of the population in Bolsward, while in the rest of Friesland they accounted for less than 10%.

From a very young age Anno Brandsma lived in his family home with a simple but strong faith, typical of a family which was very proud of its Catholic heritage. In fact, his father was a member of the parish council and president of the local Catholic party who, even in those days, fought for freedom of education and of the press. His father's dedication to this struggle would perhaps remain engraved in the mind of the future Carmelite. Of the six children in the Brandsma family, five would become religious. Other relatives, both close and distant, were also missionaries or religious in various congregations. Two relatives were missionary bishops in Africa and China.

The best known was Bishop Gorgonius Brandsma, a member of the Missionary Society of Saint Joseph (also known as the "Mill Hill Mission"). After serving in various African countries, he was appointed superior of the Mill Hill missionaries in the Congo, later Apostolic Prefect of Kavirondo in Kenya, and then Apostolic Vicar of Kisumu. He was ultimately consecrated as a bishop in 1933.

News of these relatives in such distant lands reached the humble home of the Brandsma family in the form of letters, and young Anno would listen with rapt attention and curiosity. He would listen as his relatives described their work, and those "dangerous and exotic" places would figure in the imaginings of a very astute child.

At the same time, young Anno, who suffered from poor health and physical weakness, lived intensely the simple piety typical of his family environment. He was an altar boy in his Franciscan parish. Thus, when he showed the first signs of his religious vocation, it was no great surprise to the family. He was sent to what we would call a minor seminary in Megen. There, in addition to receiving a secondary education, the young men discerned their possible religious vocation.

Anno's process of discernment was somewhat challenging. He seemed to feel called to an extreme life choice, either in the missions or in the monastic life; but his fragile health discouraged him. The family had a close relationship with the Franciscans of their parish. His parents were Franciscan tertiaries and his brother Henricus would become a Franciscan, one sister a Poor Clare, and another sister a Franciscan. Given his intellectual curiosity and ability, some of the teachers in Megen even suggested the possibility of Anno becoming a Jesuit. But the young man seemed to be looking for another spirituality, something different.

1.2. In Carmel

In the end, young Brandsma opted for an ancient Order, but one with little presence in Holland: he would be a Carmelite. It seems that the decision was greatly influenced by a long conversation with his mother's cousin, Casimiro de Boer, a member of this Order, who was about to be ordained a priest. Fr. Titus himself would declare years later that the spirit of Carmel, its distant origins lost in time, full of love for Mary, combining active life with the embers of hermit life had fascinated him. I do not doubt that. On September 17, 1898 Anno entered the historic Carmelite house in Boxmeer. A few days later he celebrated his entry into the novitiate with the customary change of name for his new life. He chose Titus as a small tribute to his father who shared the name.

Located in the province of North Brabant, not far from the border with Germany, Boxmeer was a fairly unique city in that part of the world in that Catholics historically enjoyed a certain autonomy. Boxmeer is also an important city in the history of Carmel in northern Europe, since, even in 1830, during the worst of the "exclaustrations" and "suppressions" of religious orders, this house and another in Straubing, Germany were the only ones to remain in the hands of the Order. Thus survived the Carmelite presence in both countries. At Boxmeer, Titus came into contact with the traditions of the Order. In its magnificent stained-glass windows, he discovered the legends of the Carmelite imagination; and in its beautiful cloister, small and secluded, his vocation was being forged. His novitiate lasted two years. At its conclusion, he made his religious profession. It was his only profession because until the reform that introduced the Code of Canon Law of 1917, only one profession was made and that was perpetual. It was, as he himself wrote in several letters, a very happy period in his life.

After the novitiate he began his philosophical and theological studies, first at Boxmeer and then at Zenderen and Oss. It was a weak education, with classes in the Carmelite houses themselves. But it was supplemented, when there was interest, with readings and question and answer sessions.

During this period of formation, one of the most interesting facets of Titus Brandsma was discovered: he had a true calling to become a writer and journalist. He encouraged his colleagues to collaborate on a magazine project, which was first called Bautista Mantuano (in honor of the Carmelite Renaissance poet) and later Van Nederlands Carmel ("The Carmel of Holland"). Titus produced articles of a very diverse nature, and used the pseudonym Isebrand, which years later made him smile. He also showed, as he had from a very young age, his love of poetry, writing a poem in honor of Saint Anno, the bishop of Cologne whose name he received at baptism, about a boy who had made his first communion. He dedicated this poem to his mother, Tjitsje, on the occasion of her birthday. It was an acrostic poem with the name of Teresa, since Titus considered this to be the Friesian version of his mother's name. It is a precious testimony, even in its simplicity, in which the Carmelite novice shows so his deep affection for his Lieve Moeder (Dear Mother) as well as his admiration for Saint Teresa of Avila. Love for his family helps us to understand the human and spiritual qualities of Titus Brandsma.

In fact, his first scholarly work of any significance would be about the saint from Avila. With the beginning of the new century, he began to translate from French the anthology on the life of Saint Teresa by Arnauld d'Andilly. He would publish it in 1901, a work of more than 300 pages. Nowadays it may seem strange and not very rigorous to translate the original Spanish texts of the saint of Avila into Dutch from a third language, French. However, at that time, given the scarcity of resources, texts, books, and translators, it was a relatively common practice. It was understood that it was not ideal or precise from an academic point of view. But it was the only way of disseminating classic works of Carmel (especially in a country like Holland) and making them known to a the wider public, as well as using them in the training of students. Young Carmelites in need of these texts were becoming more and more numerous in the nascent Dutch province. Brandsma's admiration for Saint Teresa led him to create an entire project to publish her works in Dutch and to produce as complete a biography as possible. But this would always be his unfinished work, postponed repeatedly, due to the various other necessities that would emerge.

1.3. In Rome and Missionary Interests

Titus' years in academic training were coming to an end. On May 28, 1904, he had already been ordained as a deacon, and on June 17, 1905, he would be ordained a priest in s'-Hertogenbosch Cathedral. Titus would never forget that date. He would always remember the enormous, unrestrained satisfaction of his parents (specially dressed for the occasion), the excitement surrounding the preparations, and the friendly advice of some superiors. For his ordination card he chose an appropriate phrase: Much will be asked of those who have been given much. Quite a prophecy! A few days later he would celebrate his first mass in the church of Saint Martin in Bolsward, his hometown.

During this period of formation, Fr. Titus was showing other important facets of his character: his independence in judgment and his personal and intellectual honesty. That he held some opinions that were too "personal"—and that he dared to express his doubts with complete honesty— would bring the penalty of having to spend a year in Oss responsible for the sacristy while his classmates left for their assignments as new priests. But if he was independent in his judgments, he was also humble and capable of putting things right, as he himself would express years later:

> Father Driessen was justified to judge my shortcomings harshly, because, being my teacher, he saw them more clearly than anyone else. He gave me helpful advice and got me to change my behavior. I owe him a debt of gratitude. But, between the two of us, there was hardly any common ground at that point, because I held opinions different from his teachings in class, always causing dispute between him and me ...

A year later, in 1906, the young Carmelite was sent to Rome, where he would earn a doctorate in philosophy at the Gregorian Pontifical University. In those years in Rome, Fr. Titus was exposed to the new currents of thought that, inspired by the encyclical *Rerum Novarum* of Leo XIII, were gradually making their way into academic world. For example, he took a course with the sociologist Antoine Pottier at the *Collegium Leonanium*. These classes made a deep impression that remained throughout his life. In this sense Rome—the academic Rome of Catholic colleges and universities—greatly enriched him. Motivated by his interest in society (which would stay with him throughout his life), he began collaborating with several Dutch newspapers and magazines, including the *Sociaal Weekblad*.

When he experienced the internationality of the Order in Rome, where he met Carmelites from all over the world, his interest in the foreign missions only increased. His province, still small but undertaking many projects with a generous spirit, was opening missions in various parts of the world. Young Titus dreamt of being sent to proclaim the Gospel; but on several occasions, and with good reason, his superiors made him give up on the idea. His fragile health had prevented him from even attempting the doctoral exams in the preceding June and forced him to delay taking them until September. He would always remember—with a spark of humor and sincere modesty—the humiliation that this represented: *Doctor, yes, but in the September commencement.*

The human and intellectual capacity of Brandsma were such that his name surfaced for various assignments and missions. Rumors even reached his Dutch province. It was said that the young Brandsma, after completing his doctorate, could stay in Rome as a professor at the new center that the Order had established in the Eternal City. Indeed, the International College of San Alberto had been built at the end of the 19th century to accommodate young Carmelites from very diverse cultures. As the Order was being restored around the world, after the harsh trials of the century that was ending, San Alberto was growing little by little. There was talk of adding an additional floor, increasing the building's capacity, and (given its magnificent location very close to St. Peter's Basilica and the Roman universities) turning it into a *studium generale.* This would be a center where young Carmelites could not only reside but also take the usual courses in philosophy and theology. To accomplish this, qualified teachers were needed; and Fr. Titus Brandsma was undoubtedly a serious candidate. A brother from the Dutch province wrote to him in confidence and asked if the rumors were true. Brandsma's response is very significant, clearly showing his open and generous missionary spirit:

> Dear Aloysius: You ask me if I will return to Holland and perhaps you are afraid that I will not. Since we are writing to each other, I would like to tell you (as you must already know) that I have never been concerned about wanting something special for myself, although of course, following the course of events, sometimes I can expect something. If the superiors think that I can be useful in Australia, Japan, Russia, or the United States, I am ready to leave early in the morning. In this regard I have not changed. In a sense, it could be

said that my ties with the Dutch province are somewhat weak, but not for lack of affection; no, quite the opposite. I even wish I could do something in that regard. But, thank God, we belong to a Catholic order, which in Greek means universal ...

Indeed, on October 26, 1909, the day after his final exam, he left Rome definitively for his Dutch province, in spite of Aloysius's fears.

II

ACADEMIC, UNIVERSITY
AND JOURNALISTIC ACTIVITY

2.1. Foundation of Schools

In October 1909 Fr. Titus returned to Holland full of plans and hopes. He would first go to work in the field of education. Thus, in addition to teaching young Carmelite aspirants at the student house in Oss where he himself had studied, he put all his energies into the establishment of Catholic schools. Neither Holland nor the Carmelites were prepared for this.

On the one hand, the Dutch State, traditionally identified with the Protestant reform, did not envisage in any clear way possibility of subsidizing Catholic schools on equal terms with the state educational programs. Fr. Titus, no doubt, could see the gap in this area and at the same time the need for schools in a Catholic environment. For him, moreover, such centers would contribute much to the very society of which they were part. There was no nefarious intention behind the move, nor any desire to restore Catholic dominance but only the wish to participate freely in the building up of a better society. Catholics could contribute, but Catholic training and the centers, which imparted Catholic values were necessary. On the other hand, the Carmelite Order was not familiar with secondary schools in the modern sense (although the Order already directed some), even if, from the time of its founding at the dawn of the 13th century, it had contributed much to the intellectual life of Europe. While this initiative on the part of the young Fr. Titus did not fail to arouse certain misgivings, it was nonetheless launched without any significant hesitation.

From these efforts emerged the Commercial School of Oss in 1919 (which would later become a lyceum) and the Classical Lyceum of Oldenzaal in 1923. Fr. Titus even managed to have a motion debated in the Dutch Parliament, and the government's decision can be considered historic because in 1926 it accepted giving grants to Catholic schools. To coordinate this, the Union of Catholic Schools was set up and was chaired by Fr. Titus until his death. This association would play an important role some years later in confrontations with the National Socialist authorities. Fr. Titus would be grateful for the supportive resistance of the Dutch state and society when the Nazi invaders tried to force Catholic schools to act against children of Jewish origin.

The young Carmelite worked at the highest levels, seeking better support from the State, the creation of additional Catholic schools, and the organizing of Catholic schools into associations. He also personally contributed to the work of the school in Oss by giving classes, replacing absent teachers, and helping as the school secretary. In addition, we have several very interesting articles on education written by Professor Brandsma. In these he reflects on the different types of teachers and students according to their motivations and their attitudes and how each of them should be treated. He also defended a more comprehensive and inclusive education which avoids the "dichotomies" of theory/practice and idealism/realism. He favors an education capable of captivating and enthusing the students and of warning them against the existential pessimism that sometimes exists in society. Fr. Titus recommended positive motivation, that the student's small successes be recognized and applauded. He promoted, in brief, an education which avoids excessive rigidity. In its pedagogical conception, the idea of "accompanying" students in their learning process and in their later lives seems very important. Fr. Titus insisted on the value of maintaining contact with former students who already live and work in the professions. Likewise, in an aesthetic mode, he attached great importance to exploring Beauty, which helps us to focus and concentrate, stimulates us to learn, and leads us toward an ultimate sense of reality. Evidently the Frisian Carmelite had some knowledge of pedagogy and even quoted, with some facility, the pedagogical thought of authors like Rousseau.

In these years of intense activity, there was no shortage of difficulties. The Dutch Carmelites continued to spread Carmel throughout the world with incredible missionary vigor. To their foundations in Brazil, were added those in Indonesia and, after the Second World War, in the Philippines. Father Titus asked again to be sent as a missionary, but for various reasons, mainly his poor health, he remained in the Netherlands. He knew how to make up for this frustration by collaborating from home with those distant missions. Thus, he organized various missionary encounters, meetings, and special collections. The most important of these meetings was the Missionary Congress of Oss in 1922, which was attended by faithful from all over the Netherlands, as well as various bishops.

It should also be noted that, in November 1933, at an International Congress on the Missions held in Amsterdam, Fr. Titus offered an interesting presentation (apparently in German) on the importance of the cloistered life to the missions. It is a valuable insight that anticipates what the Decree *Ad Gentes* of the Second Vatican Council will outline many years later (*AG*, 18, 40).

Likewise, in a radio address in 1936, Brandsma insisted on the need to pray for the missions and to manifest the unity of the Church with the missions by collaborating with other orders and congregations. In a style very typical of Professor Brandsma (always avoiding provincialism and sterile divisions), he calls for the union of forces in missionary work and shows his healthy pride in the significant contribution of the Church of the Netherlands to this work of the global Church. Brandsma cites as an example the fact that there were almost thirty Dutch bishops in various mission areas. Certainly, in the specific case of Carmel, the missionary work of the Dutch province in the first half of the 20th century was impressive.

Finally, in his famous homily on Saints Willibrord and Boniface, evangelizers of Friesland (to which we will refer later), Fr. Titus teaches how the engine of evangelizing and missionary work should be love, the search for happiness and the good of the evangelized people. This is a fundamental dimension of mission: evangelization comes from the conviction that the Gospel is a message of joy.

In one of these gatherings, his illness—that inseparable companion which had been silent for some time—reminded him again of his limitations. In 1921, while in Boxmeer on a missionary week, Fr. Titus suffered a severe hemorrhage. He remained convalescent for several months and had to leave various projects and tasks uncompleted.

2.2. At the University of Nijmegen and as Rector

Dutch Catholicism, a vital and vigorous minority, had been attempting for years to create a Catholic university, which in keeping with its religious ethos, would meet its most serious and academic needs. That long-cherished project would crystallize in the foundation of the Catholic University of Nijmegen in 1923. In a way, it was the crowning glory of the emancipation process of the Catholic Church in the Netherlands. It must be remembered that the Dutch Catholic hierarchy had only been restored in 1853 by Pope Pius IX. Known today as *Radboud Universi-*

teit Nijmegen, it welcomes more than 17,000 students and enjoys great prestige both nationally and internationally. Since 1968 the faculty of theology has included the Titus Brandsma Institute of Spirituality in honor of our Carmelite. The Institute is a leading center for the scientific study of spiritual theology.

One of those called to be a professor at the nascent university in 1923 was Titus Brandsma himself. From then, until the very afternoon on which he was arrested, Professor Brandsma devoted himself with genuine passion to the profession of teaching. He was professor of the history of mysticism and philosophy. In 1932, he received the highest honor for a teacher at the university in being appointed *Rector Magnificus*, a position he would hold throughout the 1932-33 academic year.

As Rector he worked tirelessly to improve all aspects of the university, from the purchase of books for the library, to the acquisition of funds and scholarships, from the improvement of furniture, to the creation of a newspaper for the university community, called *Vox Carolina*. However, it was not an easy year. The European political situation was becoming complicated. It was the year of Hitler's rise to power in Germany and the opening year of the Dachau *Lager*, a labor camp for prisoners in the heart of Bavaria, a few kilometers from Munich. This coincidence of dates brought Fr. Titus into a relationship, still distant yet, with these names. In several European capitals, there were student and union protests against the new German regime. In Nijmegen, as well, there were demonstrations of this sort. One of them was carried out—apparently with some disorderly behavior—by some students of the Catholic university. A majority of the teachers (and the general opinion of the city) held that sanctions should be leveled against these students, calling them communists. The Rector refused, but he did speak personally with some of the organizers. His spirit of openness and dialogue prevented him imposing sanctions, and in those turbulent years a display of that virtue was somewhat more significant than even in our own day. Likewise, there were also demonstrations on the opposite side: young people who saw in the nascent German regime an ideal of strength and patriotism and who admired its overwhelming momentum. In all of these cases, Rector Brandsma had to act calmly and serenely.

His conciliatory spirit was also useful with the teachers. There was no lack of little quarrels and jealousies. These are, of course, common in a university environment, and here, too, the Rector knew how to listen and work to bring people together, to integrate diverse sensitivities and attitudes.

One sign of the good relationship that Professor Brandsma maintained with students is that on several occasions he was invited to participate in student club meetings at various other universities. These student organizations were much in vogue at that time. The professor can be seen in several photos participating in a student party at Nijmegen University or these other universities. At one of these assemblies (in Groningen in 1935) the Carmelite gave a speech in which—without explicitly mentioning incipient National Socialism—he denounced the "heroic" model that was being proposed to young people. He offered an alternative of the "Christian hero," one characterized by forgiveness, humility, and sacrifice. Brandsma's character and dedication were unofficially rewarded when, just after he had left his position as Rector, a large group of students gathered at the Carmelite residence to cheer him on.

With regard to the university and academic life of Professor Brandsma, there is some controversy. Various opinions are put forth. For some, the many activities in which he so generously participated throughout his life would have hampered his dedication to larger research work and a more far-reaching commitment to teaching. There are a few testimonies, given during the beatification process, that point out Father Brandsma's chronic inability to say no to the constant invitations to serve on various commissions of every type. For others, Fr. Titus, without losing an iota of his academic rigor and scientific seriousness, was admired for being more versatile, less able to be pigeonholed in a particular aspect of research. For him, both teaching and research would be part of a broader and more inclusive work that we might describe as "pastoral."

This was well expressed by his former student and later colleague, the eminent philologist Christine Mohrmann, in her declaration for the beatification process. Fr. Titus was hired from the founding of the university as an ordinary professor, but in the early years he had few students. In fact, Christine Mohrmann attended some of the young professor's courses as the only student. Given his generosity, and perhaps because of his lack of assertiveness, little by little Fr. Titus was loaded with work of all kinds. In this respect, for Professor Mohrmann, perhaps Professor Brandsma did not respond to what was expected of an ordinary teacher in terms of scientific production and research. He was not considered a member of the academic elite of the teaching staff. However, Professor Mohrmann underlined his dedication to teaching, his regularity and dedication, as well as his outstanding work as Rector in 1932, a particularly difficult and turbulent period. Furthermore, in her last academic act at the University of Nijmegen in 1977, Professor Mohrmann emotionally highlighted how Fr. Titus had not only left a deep impression on her that had accompanied her throughout her life but had also brought her into contact with medieval thought. Then, with a spark of humor, the eminent professor added that yes, Brandsma lacked the solemnity and airs of importance that were then considered indispensable for university faculty. Later, we will see how he had produced, in fact, no shortage of fine research, especially in the field of the history of Dutch mysticism.

Finally, during this period in which he served as Rector of the Catholic University of Nijmegen, Titus Brandsma delivered one of the most important speeches of his life. On the anniversary of the founding of the university, the new Rector delivered his investiture lecture entitled *Godsbegrip (The Concept of God)*. In this he revealed one of his deepest intellectual and spiritual concerns: the abandonment of God by modern society, humanity's inability to discover God. With admirable intellectual honesty, Brandsma points out various reasons for this abandonment. Without ignoring the role that believers themselves have in such a rejection, the new Rector senses a new paganism involving science and technology which, although good in themselves, set themselves up as idols. This preoccupation with "neopaganism"—to which Brandsma will add in later denunciations the cults of war and violence and race—was already a reoccurring theme in his work and intellectual reflection.

2.3. Travels for Study

Throughout his university career, Professor Brandsma undertook several trips abroad to expand his knowledge as well as to give courses and lectures. Among them, apart from institutional trips as professor or Rector, his trip to Spain in 1929 stands out. His visits to Barcelona, Burgos, Avila, Madrid, Toledo, and Seville left behind pleasant memories of simplicity and sympathy in the minds of people who met him. To understand this journey, we must consider the deep admiration that Fr. Titus professed for Saint Teresa of Jesus. Some affirmed during the beatification process that he knew *Las moradas (The Interior Castle)* practically by heart. Therefore, the Dutch Carmelite paid some emotional visits to the important places in Saint Teresa's life. He proposed again to continue the Dutch translation and publication of the saint's works, as well as to write her biography—a project always frustrated by his various side jobs. This would only ultimately begin in the prison cell of Scheveningen. This trip to Spain also highlights the impression made on him by the Montserrat Monastery and the monks with whom he conversed on various topics and in various languages.

In 1932, as rector of the Catholic University of Nijmegen, Fr. Titus traveled to Milan for the inauguration of the new buildings of the Catholic University "*del Sacro Cuore*," which had been founded in 1921 (almost at the same time as Nijmegen) by the famous Agostino Gemelli. From Milan he went to Rome, where he had an audience with the pope, who gave him a rosary. Fr. Titus, in turn, would give the rosary to his mother, who died a few months later.

In 1935, the prior general of the Order asked Brandsma to give a series of lectures to North American Carmelites on various themes and aspects of the spirituality of Carmel. Fr. Titus practiced his English in Ireland where he stayed for a few months, and from there he left for the United States. The trip was mutually enriching, since if Fr. Titus showed his knowledge of Carmelite spirituality in the various conferences he gave, he too was impressed by the rise of the press in that country, something that deeply affected him. He even took the opportunity to meet with Professor Murphy, the chair of the journalism school at the Catholic University of America in Washington, DC. They discussed various issues related to the press and the possible role of the Church in this world of communications. American society made a great impact on Fr. Titus. We know this from a fascinating letter sent from there to his brother Henricus in which he comments on some aspects of the American way of life that caught his attention.

Perhaps—we can speculate—Fr. Titus was aware of the growth that newspapers such as the *Catholic Worker*, founded and directed by Dorothy Day, had achieved since it first hit the streets on May 1, 1933. It was an inexpensive newspaper (it cost only a penny) but contained ample information on the labor movement, in a tone of serious social criticism inspired by the doctrine of the Church. The newspaper was a great success, which caused amazement in some sectors. When Professor Brandsma visited the United States in 1935, there were already close to 150,000 copies in print.

Unlike Charles Dickens, who had traveled to the United States a century earlier and was greatly bothered by "the abject state of the American press" (*American Notes for General Circulation*), Fr. Titus was captivated by the American press and returned to Holland with a series of interesting ideas to put into practice.

Fr. Titus gave his first lecture (a synthesis of the series he had prepared) in McMahon Hall on the campus of the Catholic University of America. Later he repeated the same series (or one of the lectures, with slight variations) in other places such as Chicago, Hudson Lake summer camp, and Middletown, New York. One lecture series was delivered at the Monastery of Mount Carmel or Mount Carmel College in Niagara Falls, Ontario, very close to one of the most beautiful natural settings in all the world. A portrait of Fr. Titus, with a commemorative plaque, in what is now the recreation room of the Carmelite community of Mount Carmel Spiritual Centre, reminds us today that the conferences were given in that room.

Fr. Titus' awareness was shaken by the impressive spectacle of Niagara Falls, so different from the vast infinite plains of his Dutch homeland. It would inspire him to compose some of the most beautiful writings we have today about the presence of God in the world and in creation. Witnesses say that he would go to contemplate the falls, and that once, ecstatic, he exclaimed, "*I feel invaded by an overflowing joy that is above any joy.*" It does not seem strange, considering that on many other occasions, Professor Brandsma had wondered about modern humanity's blindness to the presence of God in creation and in the world. Fr Titus' response to the falls would now coincide with that of Charles Dickens, who wrote in his *American Notes* of his strong religious feelings standing before the falls: "When I felt how near to my Creator I was standing, the first effect, and the enduring one—instant and lasting—of the tremendous spectacle, was peace."

Lawrence Diether, prior provincial of the Carmelite province of the Most Pure Heart of Mary, asked Fr. Titus for the English text of his lectures. They were published under the title *Carmelite Mysticism: Historical Sketches* (Chicago, 1936). Later they were published again as *The Beauty of Carmel* (Dublin-London, 1955). They have also appeared in small pamphlets and various editions as *Carmelite Mysticism*, as can be seen in the bibliography at the end of this book.

Also on this trip, Fr. Titus participated in the profession of several Carmelites on August 15, 1935. Among them was Fr. Joachim Smet, famous historian of the Order, whose profession formula signed by Fr. Titus Brandsma is now preserved in the Titus Brandsma Memorial of Nijmegen. It was personally donated by Fr. Smet. On his return trip to Europe, aboard the *SS Washington*, he wrote a letter to his brother Henricus in which he shared his feelings about large cities like New York and Chicago. He also mentioned that over a brief stay in Great Britain he hoped to visit the town where Saint Boniface was born, Crediton, Devonshire in the South of England.

We also know that Fr. Titus traveled several times to Paris and other locations in France, to participate in conferences or study meetings. On one of these trips, like a modern-day Saint Martin, he gave his coat to a diocesan priest named Johannes Castricum who years before had started his vocational path in Carmel. During a winter trip of 1937, Titus traveled with Castricum by train to France and saw that his companion was not wearing the right clothes for the cold and unpleasant weather. So Saint Titus spontaneously and matter-of-factly gave him his own coat. Castricum, who had to remain in France during the war, would always keep that coat. When he died in 1990, it was donated to the Titus Brandsma Museum in Bolsward, where it is kept as a memento of that anecdote which, despite Its simplicity, says a great deal about the spiritual and human disposition of the Dutch Carmelite.

Of all these trips, I would highlight Fr. Titus' ability to be affected by the new places he encounters. It reminds me, in a way, of Dietrich Bonhoeffer, who was influenced by black spirituals in the United States, or by the piety of the nuns at Trinità ai Monti and the Holy Week confessions in Santa Maria Maggiore in Rome, or by bullfights in Spain. They are both wise, receptive people, who learn from new experiences—even in popular or simple areas—and who allow themselves to be enriched and enchanted by the realities they discover. Although we cannot take the time to explore it here, a whole spiritual approach is evident behind the openness of these travelers.

In this period, somewhat ironically, there were also various "trips" to hospitals and infirmaries. Fr. Titus was handicapped at times by poor health and chronic weakness, despite the apparent strength needed for his frenzied activity. Throughout these years he suffered several relapses and necessary periods of convalescence. The malady comes and goes, but it never goes away completely. It is there as a threat or—perhaps better—as a reminder of the fragility, the limits, the contingency of the projects he was undertaking. Dietrich Bonhoeffer was able to capture it in a letter to his grandmother, Julie Bonhoeffer, in which he referred to this aspect of chronic intermittent disease:

> Such a situation of real helplessness allows these people perhaps to contemplate certain realities of human existence, which deep down is defenseless, with greater clarity than what can be given to us healthy people. And precisely that sudden alternation of being healthy and falling is for such an understanding more promising than being permanently ill.

In 1937 Fr. Titus found himself seriously ill and—perhaps for the first time—admitted it to his superior. He would have to convalesce until the spring of the following year. During this period, Fr. Titus was able to read with relative tranquility and perhaps reflect on the turn of events across the old continent. Germany had strengthened and radicalized its positions. Russia, under the fierce dictatorship of an opposing ideology, paradoxically, was matching Germany. Spain was in the midst of a horrible civil war which many considered to be an experiment toward a wider war. Traditional democracies like France and England were weakened and discredited. And Italy had also contracted the warmongering fever. It did not require much pessimism to find dark clouds overhead. Professor Brandsma, however, tried to remain calm and lucid.

2.4. In the World of Journalism

On November 3, 1985, the day Fr. Titus was beatified in Rome, the RAI *Telegiornale* (Italian state-owned-television news broadcast) began with these words: *Today one of our colleagues has ascended to the Glory of Bernini.* As we saw above, Fr. Titus had, from a very young age, a great interest in the world of journalism. As a student he founded and directed small publications that, despite their simplicity, said a lot about the awakening of Carmel in the Netherlands.

Journalism, for Fr. Titus, was a true vocation in service of the truth. It is curious that some of the finest spirits of the first third of the 20th century had already reflected on the truth and its possible manipulation in the media. To give just one example, Simone Weil asked that there be courts to guarantee the independence of the media and that they not be at the service of ideologies.

As soon as he returned from Rome, in 1909, Fr. Titus began to take steps in this direction. He founded *Karmelrozen* (*The Roses of Carmel*) which would reach a circulation of more than 13,000 copies. The local newspaper of the city of

Oss (*De stad Oss*) had suffered a long-term decline, so Professor Brandsma directed it from 1919 to 1923, improving it in all respects and restoring it to its former glory.

Furthermore, Brandsma foresaw that the increasingly important social role of the press would be extended to other media. He developed this thought in a conference entitled *New Forms of Journalism*, as well as in a series of radio talks in September 1936—some of which are still preserved today. He also gave retreats to journalists, was a religious censor for the newspaper *De Genderlander*, and carried out a thousand initiatives and projects in this field.

Monsignor Jansens, aware of the commitment that Fr. Titus had made in this field from a young age, decided in 1935, to appoint him as an ecclesiastical assistant to the Union of Catholic Journalists. This would not be an easy task. Despite being of a minority confession, the Dutch Catholic press was extensive. The political situation in the country reflected the great tensions that the entire continent was experiencing. The Church was trying to maintain the difficult balance of being politically prudent yet prepared to denounce clearly certain attitudes. Titus Brandsma was not daunted. He accepted the position with humility, but when asked by a colleague about what his stance would be in the event that Germany invaded Holland, he replied with great serenity, "*I will know how to fulfill my duty.*"

The appointment was well accepted among professional journalists. They knew of the Frisian professor's disposition, his capacity for tolerance, and his generous dedication to any task. As Pope John Paul II noted in his homily at the 1985 beatification mass, regarding this journalistic work of Fr. Titus: "*Here too his work was not simply professional: many colleagues found in him a discreet confidant, a wise councilor, and a sincere friend, always ready to share sorrows and inspire hope.*"

In his speech on the day he took office, Fr. Titus insisted

that the Catholic press should bring a peaceful and conciliatory tone to the general information forum. However, such characteristics should not arise from compromises or from hiding the truth. Rather they must appear by showing the truth in all its dimensions, always with charity and respect. It was almost a prophecy—a commitment that went deeper than beautiful words that are easily spoken.

The journalists fulfilled his expectations. Titus Brandsma was not only their spiritual director, but also a friend and a liaison with the Union, in solidarity with his fellow Catholic journalists. Perhaps inspired by what he saw in the United States, he dreamed of the establishment of a college journalism chair; but that would not become a reality until several years after his death. This was a fitting goal for the Duch Carmelite. He did not see himself as an ecclesial outsider imposed on the world of the press. It was the appointment of one journalist—someone who held an ID of the *International Federation of Journalists*—who would serve other journalists.

That lofty concept of what it meant to practice journalism (to present one's own convictions humbly but firmly and honestly seek the truth without compromising one's own integrity) caused Fr. Titus to take a clear position on certain events occurring in the political and social realms. In both Germany and in Holland itself, these were principally related to gross violations of human rights in the interest of an almost hysterical defense of the fatherland and Aryan purity. Fr. Titus' comments would soon reach the Gestapo archives, as we would learn many years later.

Soon Fr. Titus was going to see how realistic some of his views on journalism had been:

> After the churches, the press is the best pulpit to preach the truth and not only to respond to those who attack us, but to proclaim the truth day after day ... The press is the force of the word against arms ... It is the power in our fight for the truth.

To sum up, we could say that there were three keys to Fr. Titus' journalistic work: the rigorous search for the truth, deep empathy with others, and the defense of the Christian faith in a world that was increasingly hostile towards it. In other words, he maintained that the Church should not be excluded from—and should defend—the freedom of expression. Consider the timeliness of this message in our post-truth world today, with its claims and counterclaims of fake news, with powerful information lobbies, and all other efforts to manipulate the truth.

This "cordial" (empathic) and rigorous (ethical) journalism of Titus Brandsma anticipated in a certain way what the first decree of the Second Vatican Council would advocate decades later. Precisely dedicated to the media of social communication, that document stated, for example, the following:

> Therefore, in society people have a right to information, in accord with the circumstances in each case, about matters concerning individuals or the community. The proper exercise of this right demands, however, that the news itself that is communicated should always be true and complete, within the bounds of justice and charity. In addition, the manner in which the news is communicated should be proper and decent. This means that in both the search for news and in reporting it, there must be full respect for the laws of morality and for the legitimate rights and dignity of the individual (*Inter Mirifica*, 5).

Fr. Titus also anticipated what great journalists and communication theorists pointed out later. In his already-classic text, *A Cynic Wouldn't Suit This Profession*, Ryszard Kapuściński identifies what he considers to be an indispensable requirement: "*I believe that to do journalism first of all, you have to be a good man, or a good woman: good human beings. Bad people cannot be good journalists.*"

II

STUDENT OF MYSTICISM AND SPIRITUALITY

3.1. Mysticism of the Cross *(the Via Crucis and the Servaes Affair)*

Throughout his life, both in the most ordinary situations as well as in the extraordinary and heroic moments, Titus Brandsma lived the advice of Saint Teresa in *The Interior Castle*: "Fix your eyes on the Crucified One and nothing else will be of much importance to you" (chapter 4 of the seventh mansion). Fr. Titus also followed the counsel of Saint John of the Cross (whom he also knew well) who in *Ascent of Mount Carmel* prescribes "setting the eyes altogether upon Christ, and seeking no new thing or anything else ..." (chapter 22 of the second part).

Due to his fragile health from childhood, and various situations that put his confidence to the test, Fr. Titus was forging a true spirituality of the passion of Christ—largely inspired by Teresian mysticism and the Rheno-Flemish spirituality with which he was very familiar.

Many testimonies from the beatification process stressed his deep, sober, and even inflexible devotion as far as external manifestations were concerned. But that devotion was rooted in the depths of his heart. It did not provoke—as one might mistakenly think—a melancholic, timid, or resigned character. Fr. Titus was the antithesis of those. He was positive, enterprising, active, and excited about the thousand tasks that waited for him, a man of good humor, with unlimited confidence in Divine Providence—even in the hardest moments.

Given his tendency towards piety and the study of the spirituality of Christ's passion, Fr. Titus was invited to evaluate personally the two "stigmatics" who enjoyed a certain fame at the time: Teresa Neumann, the famous "stigmatic of Konnersreuth," and a Protestant named Isabel Kolp. Professor Brandsma's judgment was rather curt but very respectful. First of all, he considered the subject as somewhat secondary; faith has no need for these things. Second, if something could attract people's attention, whether it was an authentic case or not, it promoted faith in the mystery of Christ. If those experiences pointed to and fostered a true devotion to the mystery of the cross, then—and only then—should they be welcomed. In fact, in the presence of the stigmatized Teresa Neumann, he was not at all impressed by the stigmata or the blood but was moved by her religious spirit.

Fr. Titus' interest in and devotion to the passion of Christ deepened after 1930 with his study of the Dutch mystics. Over the years, in his history of mysticism classes at the university, he emphasized all these figures. However, Fr. Titus will express his piety in a more personal and experiential way in the two *Via Crucis* (Ways of the Cross) which he wrote at different times and under distinct circumstances.

The first was written as a result of events which took place in 1919. In that year, the Belgian artist, Albert Servaes (1883-1966), painted a *Via Crucis* which had been commissioned by his spiritual director, the Discalced Carmelite, Jerónimo de la Madre de Dios. From a young age

Servaes had had a deep interest in religion. On one occasion he even declared of his painting. "I have only had two teachers: the Gospel and nature." Naturally, a deep spiritual harmony existed between the two. Not in vain, the Discalced Carmelite drew upon Jacques Maritain's *Art et Scholastique* (Paris 1919) in classes where he made reference to the Servaes. Students in those classes, even if they came from varying points of view, were united in feeling a need to bring art and authentic aesthetic experience closer to the religious. They were part of a cultural elite who referred to the fashionable, falsely enhanced, excessively delicate religious art of the day as kitsch.

Since Jerónimo de la Madre de Dios had seen and liked sketches by Servaes for a *Via Crucis*, he commissioned him in 1919 to draw fourteen stations for the new chapel that had just been built for the Discalced Carmelite monastery at Luithagen, near Ghent. However, when the work was finished, its harsh, realistic style caused some alarm, and some viewers were scandalized. In March 1920, before being installed in the chapel for which they were created, the drawings which were on display in the Carmelite Convent of Ghent, provoked a barrage of criticism. Among those involved were some important figures: Cardinal Mercier, Jacques Maritain, Reginald Garrigou-Lagrange, and Laurentius Jansens, the Abbot of Maredsous, one of the harshest critics of the work. The worst that could happen with Servaes' work would be for the controversy to go international or even reach Rome. His defenders, such as Cardinal Mercier, knew that if the Holy See ruled against the art, they would have to abide by the decision.

At that moment Fr. Titus came onto the scene. He had previously protected or encouraged other artists, such as the one who had created the statue of Christ the King in Oss. It is not clear why Brandsma involved himself here. We can imagine that Servaes (or more likely, Jerónimo de la Madre de Dios) knew some of Titus' writings on Saint

Teresa or on the mysticism of suffering. It seems that Brandsma first tried mediation before the superiors of the Discalced in Rome through the Postulator General of the Order, Fr. Humberto Driessen, O. Carm., his great friend; but this mediation failed. Out of pastoral sensitivity, Fr. Titus was very concerned with the painter's status as a lay person. He thought that it would be more difficult for him to take the blow of a prohibition. Then Fr. Titus made one of his typical Solomonic decisions. He expressed his understanding (despite his later criticism of them) of people who, perhaps without training, become scandalized when they see a weak, famished, too human Jesus. At the same time he asked the recently founded religious culture magazine, *Opgang*, to reproduce the *Via Crucis* in its first issue. This would give Fr. Titus the opportunity to write his famous commentary on Servaes' work. Here he will suggest in several places that the real scandal is not so much the depiction of a weak and naked Jesus, but that we ourselves, his followers, are scandalized by him.

In any case, after several unpleasant developments which we cannot stop to discuss here, the order came from Rome to remove the art. Fr. Titus asked his Discalced brother to abide by the decision, and Cardinal Mercier personally tried to console Servaes, who would later become one of the leading representatives of Belgian Expressionism. The Stations of the Cross underwent their own *Via Crucis* and passed through various hands and buyers until they reached the cloister of Koningshoeven Abbey in Tilburg.

So as not to contravene the prohibition of the Holy See, the Nuncio insisted that the Servaes stations should not be placed as an object of worship but simply as a "work of art." Today one can not only contemplate the *Via Crucis* of Servaes but can read—thanks to the controversy—Fr. Titus' meditation on each of the stations. In each he recreates—in the best tradition of Rheno-Flemish mysticism and the spirituality of Saint Teresa—the suffering of Christ in his weakness and fragility. Titus portrays this not as a masochistic or negative act but as the culmination of Christ's love for humanity and his full identification with it. He is the despised Christ, the man of sorrows, "before whom he turns his face" (Is 53:3), or the one who, "despite his divine condition, did not boast of his status as God; on the contrary, he stripped himself of his rank and took the status of a slave, passing through one of many. And so, acting like any other man, he lowered himself to even submit to death, and a death on the cross" (Phil 2: 6-11).

The second *Via Crucis* that Titus Brandsma prepared was composed in more dramatic circumstances. As we will see later, Brandsma had always felt great sympathy and devotion for the Frisian apostles, Willibrord and Boniface. The latter, according to the most widespread tradition, had died in Dokkum in the year 754 at the hands of the early Frisians who resisted evangelization. Fr. Titus had worked hard to have a chapel rebuilt in Dokkum in honor of Saint Boniface. At its inauguration, he himself preached in several languages, including the Frisian of his native land. The first stone had been laid by the dean of Leeuwarden, Monsignor Vaas, on Saint Boniface's feast day, June 5, in 1934. The chapel was constructed in a few months and was inaugurated by Monsignor Jansen, bishop of Utrecht, on August 6 of the same year. Designed by the architect H. W. Valk and built in neo-Romanesque style with "Roman bricks" (in Frisian called *Frisian Kloostermop*), Titus Brandsma liked it very much and dedicated lofty words of praise to it in a personal letter dated November 1, 1936, as well as in other documents.

Before being arrested, Fr. Titus had contacted an artist, Jac Maris (Walter Jacques Maris), to depict the Stations of the Cross. Although the work had been interrupted by the war, the prisoner Titus Brandsma, always optimistic, took advantage of his stay in Scheveningen prison to prepare the commentary which would accompany the stations. Jac

Maris would not finish his work until some years later, in 1949. It is a beautiful ceramic bas-relief with the various images of the Stations of the Cross for which Titus had written his spiritual commentary. Today both the work of Jac Maris and the commentary of Saint Titus accompany the pilgrims who pray the Way of the Cross in Dokkum. The Dokkum commentary is much shorter than the one he wrote for the Servaes paintings, but has powerful testimonial value. Professor Brandsma, Fr. Titus, the prisoner, himself joins the way of the Cross.

But the testimony in which his deep and well-rooted devotion to the passion of Christ and to the Cross is most clearly seen is in the famous poem *Before a Painting of Jesus in My Cell*, which the prisoner Brandsma wrote in February 1942 in Scheveningen prison. This poem has been translated into many languages, set to music, and used as a deep prayer for people going through difficult times.

Dear Lord, when I look on you
my love for you starts up anew:
and tells me that your heart loves me
and you my special friend would be.

More courage I will need for sure,
but any pain I will endure,
because it makes me like to you
and leads unto your kingdom, too.

In sorrow do I find my bliss,
for sorrow now no more is this:
rather the path that must be trod,
that makes me one with you, my God.

Oh, leave me here alone and still,

and all around the cold and chill,

to enter here I will have none;

I weary not when I'm alone.

For, Jesus you are at my side;

never so close did we abide.

stay with me, Jesus my delight,

your presence near makes all things right.

Experts in spirituality will find in this poem many connections with authors studied by Professor Brandsma in his classes on the history of mysticism. For example, perhaps his words resonate with these of Saint Teresa in *The Book of Her Life* (loved by Fr. Titus and translated by him into Dutch): "*Let all learned men rise up against me, let all created things persecute me, let the devils torment me, but fail Thou me not, Lord, for I have already experience of the benefits which come to him who trusts only in Thee and whom Thou deliverest*" (*Life* 25,17). Perhaps, one might also hear an echo of the *Canticle to the Holy Face* by Thérèse of Lisieux, an author that Professor Brandsma had studied and knew well.

Given this devotion to the passion of Christ and the deep experience of the Cross that he himself suffered, it is worth pondering, along with other scholars of his life, if Saint Titus Brandsma today can be called a mystic. The question raises many questions, so the answer will be complex. Fr. Titus was a very serious and reserved man in his spiritual experience. Far from anything that might seem to be exhibitionism, he always maintained a certain modesty in this area. Many times, his own experience is hidden behind his historical writings, in some emphasis placed on a certain theory, or in many of the sundry activities of his life. For this reason, he knew how to integrate apostolic activity with the spiritual in a harmonious, natural way, which surprised and aroused suspicions in some who knew him closely.

We are inclined to think that Brandsma was indeed mystical in the truest sense of the word: a believer who experiences the loving presence of God amid the vicissitudes of life, from the most ordinary to the most dramatic. Christine Mohrmann, Titus' student at Nijmegen, stated in the beatification process that the professor of the history of mysticism seemed to be talking about things that he himself had experienced or with which he was otherwise familiar. Likewise, Pieter Herman Ronge, a Protestant physician and psychologist who met Brandsma in the Amersfoort camp, pointed out during the beatification process that he had "the clear impression that [the servant of God] not only knew mysticism, but also lived it. From all his conduct it seems that the gifts of the Holy Spirit had come to full development in him."

It is difficult to think that his writings from prison, his serenity and affability (even with the guards) throughout the months in prison, and his constant invitation to maintain trust in God do not reflect a very deep spiritual experience. Well-rooted in the tradition of Carmel, Brandsma contemplates the mysterious presence of God in events and exclaims, like John to Peter on the Lake of Galilee, "*It is the Lord!*"

For Titus Brandsma, spiritual or even mystical experience is not something reserved for a special category of people. Even recognizing that it is a special gift and a grace, every believer is called to participate. In one of his lectures in the United States, he insists on this, referring to the seventeenth-century French Carmelite mystic, John of St. Samson:

> He rejected, with all the emphasis possible, the idea that the mystical life—which consists essentially neither in visions nor apparitions, nor in stigmata or levitations,

but in seeing God before us and in us—is not for each one of us.

For this reason, too, the spiritual figure of Saint Titus has always been a source of inspiration for laity, secular communities, and other groups—perhaps because they have seen in him the possibility of a deep and authentic spiritual life truly in the midst of the world. As the famous Dutch writer Godfried Bomans, a student of Brandsma at the University of Nijmegen, said, with his characteristic sense of humor, Brandsma was *"the only mystic on the continent of Europe who had a train pass and who lived his holiness in a railway compartment."* We can say, therefore, that when in 2006 in the Netherlands 40 new trains were "baptized" with the names of famous citizens and one of them received the name of *Titus Brandsma*, it was well deserved.

On February 28, 1986, in an address to representatives of journalists from Italy and abroad, Pope John Paul II emphasized this mystical and spiritual aspect of the figure of Saint Titus Brandsma. The Polish Pope stressed how, without a rich interior life, contributions like Fr. Titus' would not have been possible:

> Respect for the truth requires a serious commitment, a careful and scrupulous effort of search, verification, and evaluation ... Here the heroic figure of the Carmelite priest Titus Brandsma emerges spontaneously, whom I have had the joy of registering among the Blessed. A courageous journalist, interned and killed in a death camp for his tireless defense of the Catholic press, he remains the martyr of freedom of expression against the tyranny of the dictatorship ... These very serious and delicate tasks require an inner wealth. Titus Brandsma could not have been the teacher, the journalist, the writer who was in the midst of the maelstrom of an enormous drama, if he had not drunk from the source of an intense personal spirituality.

3.2. Main Works

Apart from his own spiritual experience, Professor Brandsma was a theorist of spirituality and mysticism. Among the many activities, publications, and fields of interest of Fr. Titus, we are going to focus only on four that we consider to be the most important and most decisive in his human and spiritual trajectory.

The subject that always attracted him the most, and in which he felt somewhat frustrated because he had never published an extensive work or devoted the attention to it that he would have liked, was the spirituality of Saint Teresa. He had always been influenced by the mysticism of the saint of Avila. There are those who affirm that his interest in her came from his curiosity about the names of his parents: his father Titus, whose name he would assume in his religious profession, and his mother Tjitsje, that is, Teresa. In 1901, while still a student, he translated from French an anthology of texts on the Saint and the life of Arnauld d'Andilly, as we discussed earlier. It was to be the first volume of the complete works in Dutch. But this would remain his great unfinished work. In 1916 Brandsma returned to the fray. For him, the lack of a translation of the works of Saint Teresa in Dutch was an especially serious deficiency in the religious culture of the Netherlands. There were some old Dutch translations, carried out in the early seventeenth century by the Jesuit Roland van Overstraten with the help of some parents from the Jesuit College in Brussels. The various editions had a rather uneven quality and reception. In addition, there was a modern translation (from the beginning of the 20th century) of *The Book of Her Life*, prepared by a "theosophist" (E. Weggeman-Guldemont); but that was widely criticized by scholars of the saint's works. The somewhat archaic language used, the poor quality of some of the versions, and the difficulty accessing these works made a new translation necessary—at least in Fr. Titus' mind.

Now the time had come to translate the saint's texts directly from Spanish. To do this, Fr. Titus formed a work team with three other Dutch Carmelites. Two years later the first volume came out, *The Book of Life*; in 1919, the *Foundations*; in 1924, the first part of the *Letters*; and, in 1926, *The Interior Castle* (a work that Professor Brandsma knew almost by heart). At that point the project came to a standstill again, in part due to the many jobs and commitments of Fr. Titus (especially at the Catholic University of Nijmegen), the transfer of Fr. Hubert to Rome, and the reorganization of personnel in the Dutch Province required by taking on various foreign missions. In a famous letter to his great friend and brother in religious life, Fr. Hubert Driessen, he confessed fraternally: "There are many things in my life that I certainly regret, but none more than that of not being able to finish the works of Saint Teresa." It is true that four volumes were published while Fr. Titus was alive, but it would not be until several years after his death that all the volumes would see the light, thanks to the Dutch Carmelite, Fr. Keulemans.

The second theme that we must highlight, and to which Brandsma devoted himself with relish, was the spirituality, culture, and language of his homeland, Friesland. As early as 1917 he had founded the Frisian Catholic Association, the *Roomks Frysk Boum*. Given that in the Friesland region the Catholic population was the minority and given that certain prejudices still existed about the "Roman" allegiance of Catholics (they were considered more Roman than Frisian), this association had as its main objective to show the Frisians that they could be Catholic without denying or neglecting their own culture. In this regard, young Professor Brandsma published many articles in the newspaper *Der Voorhoede* on the culture and piety of the Frisian Catholics. One of these articles, dedicated to Our Lady of Bolsward, is considered to be the first Catholic writing in the Frisian language in modern times. He also edited a small missal (that is, a small book allowing one to "follow the mass" which was in Latin) in his beloved Frisian language.

From the history of Friesland, Fr. Titus had a special interest in the confrontation of Saint Boniface, evangelizer of the region, with the ancient Frisian kings, leading to his martyrdom. Beyond the cultural aspect, Brandsma was attracted by the confrontation between the culture of force (represented by those barbarian kings) and the culture of love (represented by Boniface). In the decisive years of Nazism, he himself would witness this confrontation between both cultures and both worldviews, and he spoke about it in a memorable homily to which we will refer later.

In 1924 he organized the restoration of the site where, according to tradition in the year 754, Saint Boniface had been stoned to death while covering himself with the Bible. There was erected a humble chapel dedicated to the saint and later the stations of a *Via Crucis*, as mentioned earlier. It was thought that that place could be a pilgrimage center which, indeed, it did, even if Fr. Titus was not successful in engaging a religious order to take charge of it. In some of the pilgrimages in which he personally participated, he preached in the Frisian language. Despite some resentments (both political and religious), Fr. Titus managed to show those who were suspicious that this religious and cultural movement had nothing to do with an alleged Frisian separatism (his Dutch patriotism would be more than proven later), nor with a movement of Catholic exaltation against the Protestant world. He was an ecumenical man by nature—as we will see later—and in the figure of Boniface he saw a common source, a common ground for all Christian confessions that were soon to be threatened by a common enemy, what he himself would call "neopaganism."

One of the largest projects of Professor Brandsma's intellectual work was undoubtedly the so-called *Bibliotheca Neerlandica Praereformatoria* which was intended to be a great inquiry into the medieval spiritual and theological literature of the Netherlands. It was undoubtedly a very ambitious project. The idea had been gradually developing within the newly created Catholic University of Nijmegen. In principle, the teaching staff considered the possibility of publishing a collection of texts and monographs by medieval authors (especially related to Rheno-Flemish mysticism and the *Devotio moderna* reforms). The collection was to be called *Texts and Studies of Nijmegen*. But, little by little, from that original project other initiatives were born, clearly signaling that with a young and enthusiastic teaching staff the new University had a very promising future. The most outstanding of the projects was the *Bibliotheca* of which Fr. Titus published the first volume on *Devotio moderna*, one of his favorite subjects. The second project was a vast microfilm collection (still in use today) consisting of more than 17,000 manuscripts when Brandsma left the project. It was called the *Spiritual Library of Manuscripts,* and it has served as an invaluable working instrument for editions, theses, and doctoral dissertations over the years.

The fourth topic on which Fr. Titus worked ardently was Carmelite spirituality. In this area, his collaboration with the *Dictionnaire de Spiritualité* should be highlighted, in which he authored the entry "Carmes (Spiritualité de l'Ordre des)." In this collaboration he analyzes the fundamental elements of Carmelite spirituality ("l'imitation d'Élie," "la vénération de la Sainte Vierge," "vocation spéciale à la vie mystique," "exercice de la présence de Dieu," etc). Despite the obvious limitations of Carmelite historiography at that time from which it suffers, it is still a valuable contribution to the knowledge of the spiritual evolution of Carmel. It seems that, in principle, the work was commissioned by Joseph De Guibert (one of the editors of the *Dictionnaire*) from Fr. John of the Cross Brenninger, author of the famous *Carmelite Directory*. However, Brenninger recommended Fr. Titus, considering him more competent. Later he would acknowledge that Professor Brandsma's contribution far surpassed any other he might have made.

One of Brandsma's meditations that was well received and has been frequently reprinted compares Carmel to a garden. In the best tradition of Carmel, Brandsma points out the various flowers and plants and compares them to the various virtues and attitudes of Mary and typical elements of Carmelite spirituality. In fact, the Marian element was very important in his preaching and spirituality. In this sense, we should highlight a beautiful idea that he frequently repeated in his writings: we have to imitate Mary and become *Theotokoi* (bearers of God). Pope John Paul II mentioned this idea in the letter he sent to the two Superiors General (OCARM and OCD) and to the entire Carmelite Family in 2001, on the occasion of the Marian Jubilee Year, commemorating 750 years of the giving of the scapular to Saint Simon Stock. The whole passage is worth reproducing:

> This intense Marian life, which is expressed in trusting prayer, enthusiastic praise, and diligent imitation, enables us to understand how the most genuine form of devotion to the Blessed Virgin, expressed by the humble sign of the Scapular, is consecration to her Immaculate Heart (...). In this way, the heart grows in communion and familiarity with the Blessed Virgin, "as a new way of living for God and of continuing here on earth the love of Jesus the Son for his Mother Mary" (...). [As] blessed Carmelite martyr Titus Brandsma expressed it, we are put in profound harmony with Mary the *Theotokos* and become, like her, transmitters of divine life: "The Lord also sends his angel to us ... we too must accept God in our hearts, carry him in our hearts, nourish him and make him grow in us so that he is born of us and lives with us as the God-with-us, Emmanuel" (*From the report of Bl. Titus Brandsma to the Mariological Congress of Tongerloo, August 1936*).

To all these works should be added Fr. Titus' numerous articles on the history of spirituality, on the most varied topics (from Saint Augustine to Saint Gemma Galgani), as well as the preparation of a series of mystical theology congresses that took place in Nijmegen in the years 1930, 1931, 1933, and 1935.

IV

HIS SPIRITUAL AND HUMAN PROFILE

4.1. An Open Person

We use the word "open" in a very broad sense: open to new means of communication, open to different currents of thought, open to imagining new channels of evangelization. Nothing is further from Brandsma's character than closure. As a young man - as we saw earlier - he ran into difficulties due to his somewhat original interpretation of certain theological issues. This resulted in his "punishment" of being assigned to the community in Oss, while his classmates left for other destinations. These were difficult times. So-called "modernism" had aroused conflict in the Church and had stirred up a certain "witch-hunt" atmosphere. It is not that young Titus was an innovator at this early age. He simply asked himself the questions any young man might have and, with all honesty, expressed them in public. That honesty would cost him his life one day. Years later, Titus himself fondly remembered those situations, fully excusing his formator, Fr. Eugene Driessen, for the friction and theological disagreements between them.

Fr. Titus had arrived in Rome in October 1906 to further his studies. Barely a year later, Pius X would publish the famous encyclical *Pascendi dominici gregis* in which modernist errors were condemned. This encyclical had been preceded by *Lamentabili*, the July 1907 Decree of the Holy Office that condemned errors in the interpretation of Holy Scripture and dogma. With these two documents it is clear that Catholic clergy lived in a tense environment that needs to be taken into account when analyzing the situation. Curiously, due to one of those beautiful paradoxes of history, forty years later, Eugene Driessen himself would be the first to explain how the beatification process of his somewhat wayward student would begin. Driessen had resided in Rome since 1932, as the Order's General Postulator. We know of his involvement in the beatification process from a beautiful letter written in 1942 by his brother, the close friend of Father Titus, Hubert Driessen. In that letter Fr. Hubert is informing another great 20th century Carmelite, Father Bartolomé Xiberta, of the death of Father Titus and refers to his brother Eugene in this context:

> Each homily, each writing, or any of its publications, always ends with a thought to the glory and honor of Mary. A year ago, he preached the spiritual exercises for the friars in Oss and spoke only of Our Mother. It need not surprise us, therefore, that all of us see in him an example, a true saint. They all hope that he will be beatified very soon. In this sense I have already written to Fr. Eug [Eugene Driessen] and especially our nuns turn to him to obtain who knows how many things. In Heerlen they have already received a novice through his intercession and who knows how many more graces they will still obtain. They have found someone to turn to and they will not let him go.

Many times, throughout his life, Brandsma displayed his openness, this willingness to explore different paths. He was innovative in many fields that today are considered normal in the Order's apostolate but which at that time were considered risky or strange. How many times are we invited to maintain the *status quo*, to give up and avoid anything that in the long run may prove uncomfortable? Fr. Titus would not be stopped by this attitude.

Fr. Titus had an ability, which we mentioned earlier, to let himself be affected by thoughts and events. We could even describe him as a "permeable" man, in that he was capable of taking on and incorporating into his life, his way of thinking, and his piety those elements he acquired in travel, in reading, or in encounters with others. Two examples will suffice. When Fr. Titus traveled to Seville in 1929 (within the framework of his trip to Spain), he was struck by processions and expressions of popular piety which were very unlike those of his homeland. According to some biographers, our Dutch Carmelite tried to imitate these Marian processions in Holland. For example, he did so at the congress he organized in Nijmegen in 1932 for the 15th centenary of the Council of Ephesus. Similarly, on his trip to the United States, he discovered a high standard of journalism there, and this sparked his plan to organize a Faculty of Journalism in Holland. Although it would not be possible at that moment due to lack of resources, it would become a reality in 1948— unfortunately after the death of Fr. Titus.

He also demonstrated this openness when encountering a certain excess or absurd rigor, when confronted with certain legalisms that kill the spirit, thinking one is acting in the name of a supposed fidelity to the letter of the law. A pathetic example of this attitude is the anecdote about the crowded truck that transported the prisoners from the prison of Scheveningen to the Amersfoort camp. Fr. Titus was in the truck when one of the prisoners—who would later narrate the anecdote—asked one of the priests to hear his confession. The priest expressed his scruples, not knowing if he had the faculties to administer the sacrament under those conditions. Because of his doubt, Father Titus told him that he should administer the sacrament in good conscience, given the emergency situation in which they found themselves. He was giving flesh to that maxim from the Carmelite Rule that he had professed many years before: "*quia necessitas non habet legem*" (necessity overrides every law).

Also, as far as we know, Fr. Titus was open in his thought process. He was somewhat eclectic, doubting uniform and closed systems, although he held firm to the essentials. He liked to confront opinions and look for the nugget of truth they each contained. This aspect of his personality is even more striking if we consider European circumstances at the time—the tensions of exacerbated and xenophobic nationalism and totalitarianism. While Professor Brandsma was teaching his philosophy classes in college, the Hitler youth were burning books the regime considered dangerous, decadent, or subversive—books by authors such as Kafka, Marx, Freud, and Brecht. On more than one occasion, the professor from Nijmegen would recall the famous insight of the German poet Heinrich Heine, almost a hundred years earlier: "*Where they burn books, they will ultimately burn people.*"

We may conclude, therefore, that Fr. Titus was a man of deep dialogue, in the most radical and beautiful sense of the word. His exchanges with Judicial Sergeant Hardegen throughout his interrogation are, as we will see later, a precious testimony to the value of such interaction. He remained an honest, sincere, firm, and respectful man at a time when everything invited the opposite.

In the monument by the Dutch artist Arie Trum, erected at the memorial of Saint Titus in Nijmegen, this trait of Fr. Titus is presented in a very expressive way. It is a kind of open cone inside of which some of his writing can be seen. The outer surface presents a montage of photos of Fr. Titus. It is a representation of his openness, his capacity for dialogue, and, at the same time, the firmness of his convictions.

4.2. A Supportive Person

Throughout his life Fr. Titus possessed a marvelous sensitivity to the circumstances of others. He knew how to maintain that sensitivity in both ordinary events and in the tragic moments of the prisons and concentration camps. At the university he looked out for the good of his students; he was always willing to share with them something beyond strictly academic matters. According to those who lived with him, he was a great encourager of those who were in trouble—the student in distress, the father of a family who needed financial help, or the Italian colleague from the Kleve prison to whom he passed part of his already very meager daily food ration, until he was discovered and severely punished for it.

He always maintained cordial relations with Italian immigrants in Holland. During his stay in Rome to earn his doctorate in philosophy, Fr. Titus spoke—or at least made himself understood—in Italian. In the middle of his very busy life, he always found time to attend to the spiritual needs of Italian emigrants who were looking for meaningful work in Holland. He knew perfectly well the cost of this uprooting for those people. He shared with them—and more than once joked about—the memory of the Mediterranean sun amid the gray mists of the Netherlands.

It should be remembered that Titus Brandsma always worked as a priest; that is, he never abandoned pastoral work. And this sometimes brought criticism from the academic sector that was disappointed that he did not dedicate himself exclusively to research. Titus was never just "a teacher who says Mass" but rather one who felt deeply—with great responsibility and generosity—the meaning of his ministry. His attention to the cloistered nuns, his availability to his students, his confessions of the Italian immigrants and, ultimately, his openness to all, is a feature of his biography that we cannot neglect. Perhaps a good example, if only anecdotal, of the fruit of his pastoral work is the testimony of Hans A. S. Tromp, a great translator and professor of Dutch for many years at the Complutense University of Madrid. He often recalled being an altar boy for Fr. Titus and the deep impression that Fr. Titus had left on him.

Though no small thing in itself, Fr. Titus' supportive spirit is not only a virtue. It suggests a whole way of understanding faith, a whole concern about listening to those who live with us, to perceive their vital rhythms and accompany them on their journey. To this end, his concern about the likely causes of atheism in his day is significant. He did not understand why technical progress was leading people to turn away from God and lose their identity as human beings. Even in our own time, fifty or sixty years after Vatican II, it is not enough just to condemn the world, to say that everything is going wrong or that "our youth are lost." We regularly have to ask ourselves about the concerns of the people of our time—our brothers and sisters to whom we have been sent to preach the Good News. In this regard, without a doubt, Saint Titus set an innovative standard. His investiture speech as *Rector Magnificus* of the Catholic University of Nijmegen, in October 1932, developed this topic. It was a profound speech, theoretical as well as personal. Though some considered it "too pious," others (including some from the Protestant media) were moved and offered him congratulations. The new Rector confessed:

> Among the many questions I ask myself, none worries me so much as the enigma of why the person who is in the process of development, and is proud of his conquests, distances himself from God in such a remarkable way. It is astonishing that in our time of such great progress in all sorts of areas we are faced with a degradation and denial of God, spreading like a contagious disease. How is the image of God so obscured that so many are no longer affected by it? Is this only their fault? Or is something asked of us to make it shine again in brighter light over the world...?

This is certainly a complete premonition of the analysis of modern atheism that *Gaudium et Spes* will make thirty years later.

4.3. A Joyful Man

There is an interesting photo of our Fr. Titus on his trip to the United States, on the ship, accompanied by several people. They all appear to be laughing. We do not know the reason for his laughter, but we can presume it was a lively and enjoyable conversation. This was one of Fr. Titus' essential traits: a joy that springs from the depths of the soul and that permeates a lifetime, even in the most depressing situations. But we note that this joy of Saint Titus is not the kind that sometimes appears in painted representations of the saints—a theological abstract and spiritualized joy deficient in lived reality. His was a genuine physical joy—on the surface, if you like, expressive of wit and good humor. He did not lack reasons for concern or discouragement: too much work, the political situation—not only in Germany, but also in his own country where proponents of National Socialism were gradually imposing their beliefs—or the precarious health that accompanied him throughout his life. But Titus was not a complaining or languid man. Life for him was not a heavy burden. Rather, he made the most of life, accepting the Lord's call. He enjoyed his work, loved its challenges, and dedicated himself to it passionately. He was able to look at his life and find in it a thousand things to celebrate and for which to give thanks. Thus, in 1938, when weakness forced him to stay in bed for a season, suffering from a fairly serious infection, he wrote to his relatives:

> Bacilli are treacherous and use the latest tactics. They begin their offensive without an official declaration of war. But I assure you, they have nothing at all to do when the work is pressing ...

His character did not change, not even under the trials of prison and the concentration camps. He lived the truth of words he had uttered years earlier, in much more pleasant circumstances: "*Wherever I am, there must be a party.*" In this sense, we can understand some of the most familiar anecdotes from the dark final months of his life. As we will later see, in Scheveningen prison he kept a small diary, a description of his cell and the routine he developed there. He also wrote the poem *Before a Picture of Jesus in My Cell* and several letters. In one of these, he describes the moment when the door closes behind him:

> ... but when one is locked up for the first time at night in a prison cell and the door is locked behind you with keys and chains, one is stunned for a few moments, although the fact of being incarcerated at my advanced age provoked laughter rather than sadness. ... Here I am then!

It would, sadly however, never open again except to transport him to another prison.

Likewise, in one of the preserved letters which he wrote from cell 577 of Scheveningen prison, he reassures his relatives with these words:

> Psychically I do not suffer, nor do I have the need to cry or sigh. What's more, I even sing softly—in my own way, of course ...

In a letter written from the Amersfoort concentration camp on April 1, 1942, Titus welcomes Easter and refers to the deep joy it produces in him. He quietly jokes again about his famous difficulty with singing: "An Easter full of blessing to all. I jubilantly intone the Alleluia with you (you know...)." Titus certainly had not inherited much musical ability from his father, who, on winter evenings in his native Friesland, played on the piano polkas, mazurkas, and religious hymns.

In other writings, we have highlighted some connections between the spirituality of Fr. Titus and that of Thérèse of Lisieux, one figure who, despite her apparent simplicity, has most influenced the spiritual history of the 20th century. Although they are two very different saints, separated by time and space, we believe that their spiritual experiences share a series of common aspects that speak to the simplicity of what is essential. Among these aspects are a common interest in missions, attention to details, strong family experiences, and everyday spirituality. Among these we also note how both Carmelites shared a fine sense of humor that can be seen in their works and personal letters. Thus, beside Titus' *"Where I am, there must be a party,"* we could place Thérèse's *"Love is not to hide it but to enlighten and rejoice."* In company with Father Titus—now elderly and ill in prison, trying to find some humor in his captivity—we can hear Thérèse trying to rise above her suffering:

> I always see the bright side of things. There are those who take everything in the way that makes them suffer the most. The opposite happens to me. When pure suffering comes to me, when the sky turns so black that I don't see any clarity, well, I make it my joy! [*Last conversations* (yellow notebook), May 27 (n.6)].

A seasoned reader will sense the greatness of mind and the deep spirituality that hides behind this sense of humor. It is simply the fruit of abandoning the many idols that enslave and sadden us.

4.4. A Familiar Man

We have two things in mind when we say that Saint Titus Brandsma was a "familiar" man. First, he was familiar in dealing with others—close, affable, ready to start a conversation. This is constantly repeated in the minutes and documents of the beatification process. Thus, on his return from one of his brief stays in Oss, on his way to Nijmegen, he did not hesitate to invite for tea a lady whom he had met on the train and with whom he had a lively conversation. And returning one day from his classes at the University, he did not hesitate to roll up his sleeves and help push a junk cart for a man in a hurry.

But we also use "familiar" in the most proper sense of the word, that is, a man who lives close to his family, who cares for them even in the most difficult moments. We know quite a bit about the Brandsma family; they were tough Catholics, honest peasants, and humble as the Friesian lands. It was a family capable of giving five children to the Church as religious, but which, despite this, always maintained a certain character of unity and affection. We also know that the practice of religious orders could be quite harsh in this regard, insisting that the religious had died to the world and, therefore, also to family ties. Father Titus understood this, but he interpreted it in a more positive way, which is why he never felt alien to the problems and joys of his family. We find a prolific correspondence with his siblings, especially his brother Henricus, a Franciscan, with whom he maintained a fairly close relationship. Particularly striking is the birthday letter he sent him from the Kleve prison in Germany on June 3, 1942, less than two months before his death. Not without a certain melancholy, Brandsma reminds him of "*happy times of days gone by.*" Unfailing in his optimism, Titus encourages Henricus once more, "But, those good times will return, and I hope soon..."

We also note the delicacy which Titus shows towards his family. Attentive to family events, even from the Dachau concentration camp, he sends birthday wishes to his siblings and niece and nephew. He is always careful not to worry them about his health problems or with the situation in jail, but is always ready to give encouragement. His behavior towards his widowed mother is also sobering. While living in Nijmegen, amid the feverish activity that we have seen, he always found opportunities in his busy schedule to take his mother with him or accompany her on long walks around the city to visit family and friends, thus relieving her loneliness. Titus was aware of his responsibility towards this woman who had given five children to the Church. His brother Henricus spoke about his brother's letters to one of Titus' first biographers:

> No one knew how to write more cordial letters than him. He was interested in everything: the school grades of our niece and nephew, the health of our parents and siblings, the weather, if the hay grew, how the cattle were doing. Dad always found him a great help.

In the comparison of Titus Brandsma and Thérèse of Lisieux mentioned above, we revealed how both Carmelites shared an intense experience of family that marks their respective spiritualities. The family dimension of young Thérèse's spirituality—her close relationship with her father and her sisters, the correspondence with her relatives—is well known. Hans Urs von Balthasar, the Swiss theologian, held this opinion in his extensive study dedicated to Thérèse of Lisieux. He pointed out that Thérèse's family lived the atmosphere of the domestic Church, in the most radical and profound sense of that expression. This enabled Thérèse to saturate every aspect of her life of faith and her religious consecration with that family spirit. Despite the rigidity of religious observance in those times, stiffened by certain lingering Jansenist beliefs, Thérèse never breaks ties with her family, although she will live with them in a different way. For her, religious life does not mean repressing your heart, nor merely living as a single person, but rather a broadening of horizons. It is not dying to the family, but rather incorporating the convent, the Church, all of humanity into our family. For this reason, Thérèse stated decisively in one of her letters addressed to Céline Maudelonde: *"The bars of Carmel have not been made to separate the hearts that only love each other in Jesus, but rather serve to strengthen the ties that unite.*" (Letter 159) It stands to reason that from such a family some vocations to religious life would arise, as would happen a few years later to the Brandsma family of Dutch Friesland.

4.5. A Man of Spiritual Discretion

Many of Saint Titus' prison companions, in their declarations for the beatification process, agree that he was a man of prudence, discretion, and civility in his dealings with others, capable of combining simplicity and spontaneity with a cultured manner. These traits of his character also permeate his spirituality.

We have already seen how little Fr. Titus respected fanaticism and the excesses of character. Several times he was called to give his opinion on various cases of stigmatics and visionaries. In these cases, his position was always very prudent, with a skepticism that was not hurtful or disrespectful but always aware of how unimportant these manifestations are in the experience of a mature faith. As we saw above, he traveled to Bavaria in 1930 to learn about the case of Teresa Neumann, the stigmatic of Konnersreuth, and also learned about the case of Elisabeth Kolb. Both cases led him to write some reflections on the subject.

Moreover, given a reputation for holiness that Fr. Titus was acquiring in Nijmegen, the rumor spread that he had experienced certain apparitions of either Saint Teresa of Avila or Saint Thérèse of Lisieux—biographers are unclear as to exactly which saint was involved. But when the news reached Titus himself, he responded, without any of his characteristic modesty, with a loud laugh.

Fr. Titus was quite sparing when it came to narrating his own spiritual experiences. Despite being a deeply outgoing man, he demonstrated a certain modesty; in his case, extroversion is not linked to superficiality. He also saw prayer as something intimately linked to daily life. "*Prayer is not an oasis in the desert of life, it is the whole of life*," he once said. Some of his fellow teachers, and even his disciples who would later become illustrious teachers, have insisted on this: he was a man who lived in deep union with God in his daily life and work. Take as an example the spiritual advice that he gives to his Poor Clare sister: "*Do perfectly your small duties, even the most insignificant. It is something simple. Follow the Lord as a child follows his father.*"

In this sense, some authors have questioned the mystical spirit of Fr. Titus. I think that when we look at his writings while in prison there can be no doubt. It is, of course, appropriate to consider what we mean by "mysticism" and what kind of "mystic" we find in Titus Brandsma. We could speak of a mysticism deeply incarnated in the human being, in which God himself is contemplated, in the truest sense of the word. It is not a contemplation that consists of only looking heavenward and forgetting or neglecting what is below. It is not even a question of bringing what is contemplated to others (the famous adage of Saint Thomas: *contemplata aliis tradere* [S.Th. II - II, q. 188, a. 6.]), recognizing the step forward that this idea implies in the conception of contemplation, which thus ceases to be an individualistic or narcissistic joy. Rather, it is a matter of contemplating within reality itself (by the principle of incarnation) the mysterious presence of God. Perhaps that is where contemplation and compassion meet naturally.

Finally, it should be noted that Saint Titus was a deeply "observant" man, to use a term that may be somewhat out of date today but which was fundamental to the spirituality of religious life in those years. Community life, the divine office in community, moments of work and recreation were fundamental to his life. Let us remember that the Dutch Province was greatly influenced by the mentality of the Reform of Touraine, a Carmelite spiritual movement of the 17th century. This reform was characterized by its emphasis on religious observance. Nowadays it is relatively easy to combine an active life with life in religious community; but at that time, and especially considering the type of activities in which Professor Brandsma was involved, it could not have been easy. However, he was very clear in his priorities, certain that the apostolate should be the fruit of an interior life, carried with love out into the world around us.

4.6. A Man of Ecumenism

In Dublin's Carmelite College of Terenure, a small chapel is dedicated to the Christian martyrs of our day, regardless of their confession. It is officially dedicated to Saint Titus Brandsma and also includes the names of Edith Stein, Dietrich Bonhoeffer, Maximilian Kolbe, Bishop Oscar Romero, and Martin Luther King, Jr. In Titus Brandsma an ecumenical model was found that could bring together characters of such powerful stature.

Fr. Titus had a truly ecumenical character, not only in the denominational sense of the relationship between Christian Churches, but also in a more general way. He was a conciliatory man by nature, an advocate of breaking barriers and establishing dialogue wherever it was needed. As a good journalist by vocation, he believed in the magical power of the word to overcome apparently insurmountable obstacles. In a way, Brandsma understood the consequences of the famous thought of his 16th century Carmelite sister, Mary Magdalene de Pazzi. She posited that God is *communicative.* And so must we be, in order to collaborate in God's sacred work.

In some of the jobs he took on as a journalist, he earned an affectionate nickname, "the conciliator." In Dachau, too, given the unending stress of that hellish place, he found himself mediating fights and disputes on quite a few occasions. The Austrian psychologist, Viktor Frankl (himself a prisoner in camps such as Theresienstadt, Auschwitz, and eventually two satellite camps of Dachau), notes in *Man's Search for Meaning* that "irritability" was one of the essential characteristics of life in the prison camps. It was hard to keep a cool head, let alone to mediate disputes that would erupt over anything—a piece of bread, a misunderstood gesture, a cigarette.

Perhaps, we can also see Titus' ecumenical spirit in his interest in Esperanto. It was a language created in 1859 by Dr. Ludwik Lejzer Zamenhof, a Jewish ophthalmologist from Białystok, in a region of the Russian Empire which is now part of Poland. It was an area of old Europe in which varied ethnic and religious groups lived together, each with their own language. Zamenhof created Esperanto with the idea that it would become a universal language. He hoped that it would overcome barriers and divisions—a neutral language that would not arouse suspicions or prejudices. The name of the new language comes from the pseudonym with which Zamenhof signed his first grammar (entitled *Lingvo internacia. Antaŭparolo kaj full lernolibro*). It says much about his beautiful idealism: *Doktoro Esperanto,* the "hopeful doctor." Zamenhof died in Warsaw in 1917 after having received several decorations and international recognition; but he had seen the European continent bleed nearly to death in an unprecedented war of vast dimensions. Over the years, Esperanto has had a mixed reception. Not widely used today, it was very successful in its first decades in Eastern European countries and was popular in anarchist circles that advocated an internationalism to transcend borders and divisions. Also, in the Catholic Church and in other Christian confessions, the significance of Esperanto has been appreciated. Pius X blessed Esperanto and predicted "a great future." The Pope has included Esperanto among the languages used for the *urbi et orbi* blessing, and Vatican Radio broadcasts some programs in this language.

We know of discussions with his fellow Carmelite and good friend Hubert Driessen, who was much more skeptical about it and doubted that an artificial language could ever be successful. Although we cannot discuss this further now, we do know that Brandsma participated in several international congresses, that he was aware of a religious bibliography that was being translated into Esperanto, and that he was a member of the Commission for the Ecclesiastical Dictionary of Esperanto. It is not surprising that Professor Brandsma, an ecumenist and advocate of mutual understanding, became enthusiastic about this language and promoted it as a means of bridging differences and creating dialogue.

Among the testimonies presented in the beatification process, there were many Dutch and German Protestants who, perhaps paradoxically, were the most strident in witnessing to the sanctity of Saint Titus. Among these are some which date from the harsh months of the prisons and camps. We should especially note the deep relationship that he established with two young Protestants, Cornelius de Graaft and William Oostdijk, who shared a cell with him during his second stay in Scheveningen. He shared long talks with them in the midst of tedious prison life and even fostered their small ecumenical celebrations on Sundays. But this is only one of many testimonies of Protestants who shared these terrible moments with him.

In fact, we do not exaggerate to say that, in more than a few cases, the sinister world of the concentration camp was converted into an ecumenical meeting place. Many survivors bear witness to this. Among them, I would highlight an author of the stature of Jean Guitton, who, in an ecumenical diary titled *Dialogue avec les précurseurs* dedicates several pages to the subject and recalls the great figures in the history of ecumenism in the 20th century—Halifax, Brother Roger, Cardinal Mercier. Guitton notes the importance of the dramatic experience of the *Lagers* in the development of ecumenism, where a rudimentary week of Christian unity was even held clandestinely. Our Saint Titus participated naturally in this beautiful "catacomb ecumenism."

Fr. Albert Urbanski, a Polish Carmelite who spent several years in Dachau, also witnessed this and alludes to these ecumenical gestures in his diary entitled *Duchowni w Dachau* (*The Clergy in Dachau*):

> In addition to Catholic priests, there were also clergy of other confessions in our block, namely Orthodox and Mariavites. The Germans called everyone *Pfaffen* (clergymen). In the end, the new Orthodox ecclesiastics from Yugoslavia were assigned to our Polish block. Every Sunday they organized religious services in our block according to their rite with the singing of melodies in Old Slavonic. We even invited them to give us lectures on the subject of Orthodox relations with the Catholic Church.

It was not only a relationship of Christian fraternity, charity, and solidarity, but also of the deep and hopeful joy of being able to share the lordship of Christ in that kingdom of evil, barbarism, darkness, and death which was the world of concentration camps.

Many years later, referring to this ecumenism of martyrdom, Pope Saint John Paul II began his encyclical on ecumenism, *Ut Unum Sint*, with these beautiful words:

> The courageous witness of so many martyrs of our century, including members of Churches and Ecclesial Communities not in full communion with the Catholic Church, gives new vigor to the Council's call and reminds us of our duty to listen to and put into practice its exhortation. These brothers and sisters of ours, united in the selfless offering of their lives for the Kingdom of God, are the most powerful proof that every factor of division can be transcended and overcome in the total gift of self for the sake of the Gospel.

The witness of one of the Protestant ministers whom Brandsma met in the Dachau camp says much. These pastors were invited to testify later in the beatification process by Fr. Adrian Staring, vice-postulator for the cause. The words could not be more meaningful and fraternal, since, on the one hand, they show their reservations regarding beatifications and canonizations (in the best Reformed tradition of opposing "works" or "merits") but, on the other, they recognize the example of Father Titus and bless God for his life:

Reverend and most learned Mr. Staring:

You have already indicated in your letter that we as Reformed have certain reservations regarding beatifications and special canonizations. This does not, however, prevent me from gladly sending you some of my impressions. I was in very close contact with Fr. Titus, as, for example, was another Protestant pastor, Hindelopen of Amstelveen. If I'm not mistaken, they were both in the same transport that took them from Amersfoort to Dachau. Later I had a little more contact, although he was closer to Arnold van Lierop, chaplain of the Catholic Organization of the Press (...). I can offer full assurance of the following: all colleagues spoke with great esteem and respect for Titus Brandsma. His well-known poem reflects his full trust in God (...). I still remember finding him in the bathroom a day or some days before his death. At that moment he knew he had to go. He was totally at peace and accepting of his situation. He gave me his last cigars. I cannot tell you much more news. I can confirm, however, all that you already know. Finally, as a Protestant pastor, I can testify that Titus Brandsma was a son of God by the grace of Jesus Christ. I hope to see him again in heaven.

But the ecumenical spirit of Saint Titus was not manifested only in this extreme situation. Earlier in his years of full activity there appeared that desire not to injure "the Protestant brother," a very delicate relationship in these countries of Catholic-Protestant coexistence. Thus, when organizing a Marian Congress in 1932 to celebrate the 15th centenary of the Council of Ephesus, Fr. Titus immediately wrote to clarify its intention, trying to avoid any sense of Catholic exhibitionism and underlining how devotion to the Blessed Virgin brings us closer to the Gospel and to Christ. Once again, Brandsma was ahead of Vatican II. Compare his stance with the famous text from *Lumen Gentium* 67, which I think is worth reproducing:

> Likewise [the Sacred Synod] exhorts theologians and preachers of the divine word to abstain zealously both from all gross exaggerations as well as from petty narrow-mindedness in considering the singular dignity of the Mother of God. Following the study of Sacred Scripture, of the Holy Fathers, the doctors and liturgy of the Church, and under the guidance of the Church's magisterium, let them rightly illustrate the duties and privileges of the Blessed Virgin which always look to Christ, the source of all truth, sanctity, and piety. Let them assiduously keep away from whatever, either by word or deed, could lead separated brethren or any other into error regarding the true doctrine of the Church.

Some have also interpreted along this same line Saint Titus' interest in studying and spreading a devotion to Saint Boniface, the evangelizer of his native region, Friesland. It would be like trying to find the roots of a common faith, looking for what unites rather than what separates. Likewise, we know that, in several of his defenses of Dutch Catholicism against Nazi power, he does not forget to expressly cite his Protestant brethren. All this acquires a special significance when we consider that he is some years away from the Vatican Council and that ecumenical sensitivity in his Catholic world was not yet highly developed.

We cannot forget his activity in favor of the so-called *Apostolate of Reunification* with the Orthodox Churches, to which he dedicated a lot of time and energy. The movement was relatively widespread in the Dutch dioceses, within the framework of a still incipient Catholic ecumenism. Fr. Titus became secretary general of this movement and can be seen from the testimonies of the beatification process, it seems that he took on the role with great enthusiasm and tried to recruit friends and family for said apostolate. As a result of this interest, we must mention the founding of an Oriental Institute at the University of Nijmegen, as well as his close friendship with the Patriarch Terzian of the Armenians who, on more than one occasion, was welcomed into the Carmelite priory of Nijmegen.

One could even speak of a certain "ecumenical spirit" (although, obviously, in another sense) in Fr. Titus' attitude toward Discalced Carmel. Of course, he never allowed himself to be carried away by disputes of little importance, nor by absurd animosities. In response to a question from Godfried Bomans, a well-known Dutch writer, about whether he preferred to go shod or unshod, Fr. Titus jokingly replied that he was trying to combine both possibilities—shoes by day and barefoot by night. The question from the writer had been provoked by the enthusiasm with which Professor Brandsma spoke of Saints Teresa and John of the Cross.

Likewise, in his conferences in the United States and Canada, he dedicated two sessions to Teresa and John of the Cross respectively. The one dedicated to the saint of Fontiveros began with these words:

> It is a great joy for me, a Carmelite of the mitigated branch, to be allowed to take part in the chorus of praise in honor of Saint John of the Cross, who was, along with Saint Teresa, the reformer of our Order. It is a special cause of joy for me, to have this opportunity to add my small contribution to his glory and to be an interpreter of what I am sure that all Carmelites of the mitigated observance see, as I do, in this hero of Carmel. [...] Certainly we do not look at him, as did the prior of the monastery of the Ancient Observance of Segovia, as a sign of opposition, but rather as a bond of unity, which brings us all together.

V

OPPOSITION TO NAZISM

5.1. First Clashes with National Socialism

On November 11, 1931, Fr. Titus gave a lecture at the *Bergkerk* in Deventer entitled *Peace and Love for Peace*. Various civil authorities from the city, as well as a mixture of other people, were present in the audience. During the conference, in addition to criticizing those who demanded excessive reparations to Germany which would provoke an aggressive economy and an expansionist policy in Germany, Professor Brandsma warned of the mentality that was being gradually imposed. It was a defeatist mentality that would begin to think of war as something inevitable and therefore convenient to prepare for. Moreover (and here he refers to the type of thought which gestated National Socialism almost simultaneously), according to Fr. Titus "there is the conviction—it is even openly proclaimed—that the principles of peace and love are useless in society. It is necessary to be strong in the struggle for existence, and it is necessary to be so because the law will be the one that is stronger." Faced with this and inspired by some phrases from *Quadragesimo anno* of Pius XI (an encyclical promulgated only a few months prior), the Dutch Carmelite proposes the model of Christ—and peace as a distinctive feature of the Christian life.

On October 17, 1932, Father Titus Brandsma was appointed *Rector Magnificus* of the Catholic University of Nijmegen, which carried a one-year term. For this occasion and to commemorate the ten-year anniversary of the university, he delivered a speech already alluded to. In this address, he took up the question of "the notion of God" (*Godsbegrip*). Without expressly mentioning Nazism, which was already becoming an important political force in Germany (in the following year Hitler would be elected as chancellor), Fr. Titus wondered why modern people (technical, developed, and cultured beings) distance themselves from God with all that this implies. His speech received mixed reviews. For some it was a masterpiece. For others it was too pious. However, it contained an urgent question which was prophetic for that period in time. Looking back, we can see that the question is still relevant today.

After reviewing various historical images of God, especially in Central Europe, Professor Brandsma warned of certain dangers which the keen reader will recognize as a criticism of totalitarian systems—explicitly communism, but implicitly the incipient Nazism. It was not easy to have such a lucid and prophetic vision at that time. Let us not forget that a year later Heidegger would be appointed Rector of the University of Freiburg im Breisgau, and that his speech (though it has been subject to much interpretation) did not hold back from praising the National Socialist government's new education laws and its fiery nationalistic propaganda (German *dasein*, German destiny, German youth, and such). The speech of Fr. Titus, however—with, no doubt, an intellectual framework less developed than that of the great German philosopher—warns of something that Heidegger did not realize: that the perceived absence of God (both quote Nietzsche) becomes an invitation for humanity to take God's place. It is the fearsome possibility that by establishing themselves as gods certain humans will assume mastery over the lives of others.

To fully understand Titus Brandsma's confrontation with Nazism, it is helpful to frame his opposition to it within the Church's broader conflict with National Socialism. This has not always been appreciated. We will consider here some elements of that struggle which, in all probability, influenced the thought and action of Professor Brandsma. One is the Holy Office's condemnation in February 1934 of Alfred Rosenberg's book, *The Myth of the Twentieth Century*. Another is the first document of the Dutch episcopate against Nazism in 1934, which would be followed by other highly critical documents and letters. There are also the direct confrontations with National Socialist authorities by bishops like Von Galen of Münster and Faulhaber of Munich. And there is in March 1937 the encyclical of Pius XI, *Mit brennender Sorge,* to which should be added the letter against Italian Fascism published several years earlier. Certainly, the positions against National Socialism were not monolithic within the Catholic Church or in society in general. There were vacillations, different ideological nuances, vagueness, and even complicity. However, Fr. Titus Brandsma's convictions should not be viewed in singular isolation. Rather, his position was firmly located within that of the Church—especially the Church in the Netherlands—against Nazi approaches and policies.

5.2. Tension Builds: Two Worldviews

Practically from the first moment, Adolf Hitler's National Socialist government had turned its attention to the Jews. Long before the anti-Semitic laws of September 1935, known as the "Nuremberg Laws," the Nazi government had already promulgated a series of laws and regulations that aimed to limit the action and influence of Jews across broad sectors of the economy and throughout German culture and society. Slowly but inexorably, Nazi power was reducing the rights of the Jews. This was reinforced by a clever propaganda program that blamed Jews for all the ills of German society: the economic crisis, unemployment, and even the defeat in the First World War, despite the fact that not a few German Jews had been distinguished for their valuable service in that war.

These measures did not go unnoticed by the best minds of the time. Thus, in Holland, a group of university professors, liberal politicians, Protestants, Socialists and two Catholics (Henri Poels and Titus Brandsma) compiled a small text against the treatment of Jews in Germany. Very briefly, each author expressed their opinion about these unjust discriminatory measures which were unacceptable if Germany wished to play a prominent role in in modern Europe. One thought from the Carmelite professor was more than explicit in this regard: "*What is being done against the Jews in Germany is an act of cowardice.*"

These opinions did not go unnoticed by the media sympathetic to Nazism. Thus, the newspaper *Fredericus*, accused the "cunning professor" of defending the Jews, who were nothing more than "bandits" and should be treated as such. Other related newspapers, such as *De Volksche Wacht* and *De Knuppel,* branded the text's authors as communists; and some pamphlets repeating these accusations appeared even in Nijmegen. This small Dutch publication appeared on certain lists of forbidden books that circulated among the ranks of National Socialism.

To make matters worse, a branch of the National Socialist party— the NSB (*Nationaal-Socialistische Beweging in Nederland*)—was present in the Netherlands as of 1931. Founded by Antoon Adriaan Mussert, it was not a popular party. In 1939 it had four seats in parliament, representing just over 4% of the population. Closer to Italian than to German fascism, Mussert longed for the glorious past of the Netherlands, that is, the seventeenth century, after independence from the Hapsburgs of Spain and the Holy Roman Empire. His approach was generally more anti-Catholic than anti-Protestant, although he would end up openly confronting all Christian confessions. The party also supported several parallel and sometimes paramilitary associations that were in many cases beyond Mussert's control, which made them even more dangerous. He went on to create his own political police, a Dutch version of the infamous German SS. Internal disputes soon arose within the party between German-inspired fanatics and the more nationalistic Dutch—as well as struggles among individuals with unlimited ambition. In any case, the NSB, to which Brandsma will later refer in one of his prison writings, became the antenna of Nazism in the Netherlands. It oversaw the creation of blacklists in which the Carmelite and Catholic University of Nijmegen professor, Titus Brandsma, was listed "on his own merits."

From this confrontation until the day of his arrest seven years later, Professor Brandsma always included a philosophical-theological analysis of National Socialism in his lessons. He understood it as an ideology that exalted two myths: that of the state and that of the Aryan race. It degraded the dignity of the human person, which is not an absolute function of the state. Nor does that dignity depend upon the color of one's skin or any other secondary factors. For this reason, it was obvious to Brandsma that it was an anti-Christian ideology, unacceptable to any mature believer. But, knowing the character of the professor, we can intuit yet another reason for his opposition to Nazism. He believed that people are somewhat eclectic by nature, open to dialogue, suspicious of any dogmatism that distorts the truth. One must necessarily confront any ideology which offers a single, universal explanation of everything and everyone—which overwhelms consciences and denies every trace of freedom, ingenuity, or creativity. It is a pity that many of these typed-up lessons have been lost. Some were probably hidden by Fr. Titus himself, while most were hastily grabbed up by Gestapo agents on the day of his arrest.

On July 16, 1939, Fr. Titus participated in a Frisian cultural-religious event. He himself preached at the Eucharist in honor of Saint Boniface († 751) and Saint Willibrord († 739), the two Anglo-Saxon monks who had converted Friesland to Christianity. The homily was in essence a hymn to love, in contrast to those who—in the name of power and the false exaltation of an *Übermensch*—considered it weak and degenerate. As Christians, Father Titus pointed out, we firmly believe in the power of love that, despite appearances, will always end up winning. It is worth reproducing some of this homily in which the Dutch Carmelite places the Christian concept of life, one based on love, in opposition to the neo-pagan concept:

> We live in a world that condemns love as a weakness to be overcome. It is not love, some say, that must be cultivated, but one's own strength: that each one be as strong as possible, and that the weak perish. They are the same ones who affirm that the Christian religion, proclaiming love, has already fulfilled its time and must, therefore, be replaced by the old Germanic power. Yes, unfortunately. They come to you with this doctrine, and there is no lack of dupes who accept it willingly. Love is not known. "*Amor haud amatur,*" Francis of Assisi said in his time, and some centuries later, in Florence, Saint Mary Magdalene de Pazzi rang the bell of the Carmelite monastery in ecstasy to announce to the whole world how beautiful love is.... As much as neo-paganism repudiates love, history teaches us that we, with love, will also defeat this new paganism. No, we will never renounce love, and love will reconcile the hearts of pagans ... and no matter how much an ideology strives to repudiate love and condemn it as a weakness, the living testimony of this love will convert it always in a new force capable of conquering and uniting the hearts of men.

Once more, the preaching of Fr. Titus did not go unnoticed. The *De Knuppel* newspaper again dedicated an article to him with a very expressive title, "King Radboud or Professor Brandsma?" This showed the paper's disdain for the exaltation of those two Saxon monks and not the figure of King Radboud who had opposed Christianity—a symbol of Germanism, of race, of everything that had been degraded by Christianity. It was the confrontation, already open and without dissimulation, between the glorification of the Germanic race, personified in this high medieval king of the Frisians, over Christianity, presented as a foreign import from the Irish and English monks—the cause of the degeneration of ancestral values. It is evident that a different degeneration (philosophical, moral, and political) greatly concerned Professor Brandsma, since he had given a speech shortly before, in October 1936, on the mistreatment of animals, a subject that seemingly had little to do with the question of National Socialism. He insists: "*I know well that we are living a time in which new philosophical theories condemn love ...*"

The major Christian thinkers of that time (Dietrich Bonhoeffer, for example) understood very well that this was an open struggle between National Socialism and Christianity. But it is fair to acknowledge that many members of the Christian churches did not know how to reflect at that level, nor could they comprehend the consequences and repercussions of this confrontation.

As we have pointed out, in 1938 Pope Pius XI published a very harsh encyclical against National Socialism. The pontiff highlighted the major, pernicious errors of this ideology and the dangers to which it could lead. The pope viewed the rise of these ideologies with a burning concern that gave the encyclical its title (*Mit brennender Sorge – "With Burning Concern"*). He was aware of the enormous sacrifices that would be involved in resisting this machinery. For this reason, Pius XI, in number 13 of the encyclical, thanks all those who bravely confront this neo-paganism of which Fr. Titus also spoke:

We thank you, Venerable Brethren, your priests and

Faithful, who have persisted in their Christian duty and in the defense of God's rights in the teeth of an aggressive paganism. Our gratitude, warmer still and admiring, goes out to those who, in fulfillment of their duty, have been deemed worthy of sacrifice and suffering for the love of God.

One last indication—less known at the time, but perhaps more significant for understanding Professor Brandsma's thought—is found in a letter that he sent to Professor Bellon, then Dean of the Faculty of Theology at the Catholic University of Nijmegen. In it, Brandsma shows his concern for what he considers the greatest danger to Dutch Catholicism: the theories that culminate in National Socialism. Given its brevity, it deserves to be reproduced in full:

Dear colleague:

In response to your letter of November 30, I inform you that, in my opinion, the Catholic religion in our country is weakened and threatened by a series of theories that culminate in German National Socialism and that find their maximum expression in it. This influence could be stopped in the best possible way, exposing, on the one hand, the National Socialist theories, and their philosophical origins (especially the philosophy of Nietzsche), as well as their dire consequences; and, on the other hand, clearly highlighting (positively and enthusiastically) the value of the human person, both in the natural and in the supernatural order. In answer to your question about what we have actually done about this, it seems to me sufficient to inform you that during the past academic year, in my course on the history of philosophy on current philosophical thought I have given several lessons about National Socialism. Seen from the philosophical point of view, and likewise, in my course on the philosophy of history, I have talked for a whole year of the growth and development of National Socialism as a typical example of reactionary thinking.

I am gladly at your disposal for further clarification. Your servant in Christ.

Fr. Titus Brandsma, O. Carm.

At the same time as this confrontation, pressure was increasing both on the Jews of Germany and among the nations of Europe. This made war almost inevitable. In September 1939 Germany invaded Poland, threatening the entire continent, including, of course, the peaceful and prosperous Netherlands.

5.3. Catholic Schools and Jewish Children

On May 10, 1940, the fears of the Dutch population were confirmed. The government of the Third Reich, under the pretext of protecting these nations from the French and English, invaded the Netherlands, Belgium, and Luxembourg. In the Netherlands, the invasion was completed in days, if not hours. The powerful German war machine found no difficulty in crushing the small Dutch army and dominated the country in its *Blitzkrieg* (lightning war). Fr. Titus celebrated Mass that morning while trying to maintain a minimal calm in these dramatic circumstances.

The early days of Nazi rule offered false hope that the invading power would be respectful of the Dutch. It was not to be. In a completely flat country without mountainous refuge, with a hard working and peaceful people, it was difficult to imagine an armed resistance. The Germans were aware that the real resistance from the Dutch would be more intellectual and spiritual than military. For this reason, from the beginning they set a clear objective: to leave in the hands of the Dutch those tasks which were merely technical and bureaucratic. This provided a sense of normalcy that did not frustrate the spirits of the Dutch. Then the Nazis would take firm control of the media and education, and would, little by little, transform them into the means by which to "convert" totally the Netherlands to National Socialism and, eventually, to the Third Reich. This *crescendo* in the repression of the Dutch people did not only occur in the press or education. For example, meetings of the "Apostolate of Reunification," about which Titus was so enthusiastic, were forbidden. Marian processions organized by the Carmelite, among other religious and devotional acts, were also prohibited

It would be in the fields of education and the media, however, where the repression was most severe, since the occupying government understood their importance in controlling a country. This is where, logically, the figure of Fr. Titus comes in. As we have seen, in both communications and teaching, he was a very prominent figure in the Netherlands. In regard to education, the government led by the Austrian Arthur Seyss-Inquart began by diminishing the rights of religious workers dedicated to education. For example, salaries were limited, and they could not hold management positions. Fr. Titus, who had been the president of the Association of Directors of Catholic Schools for several years, intervened with determination. He informed the directors of the measures that were underway and of those that could soon be imposed. He visited schools, contacted various ecclesiastical personalities (especially Archbishop De Jong with whom he would continue to maintain a very close collaboration), and personally visited Professor J. Van Dam, secretary of the Ministry of Education from which these regulations were issued. Van Dam promised Brandsma that he would take the case into consideration.

Although it goes beyond our subject, the conflict was much broader. In fact, the so-called Cooperative of Educators (a pro-Nazi group) publicly and without and pretense decided that the school should be at the service of the race and the country. Schools that did not comply with this ideology should gradually disappear. Logically, the Dutch episcopate (already very active in its rejection of National Socialism) was totally opposed to this educational ideology.

But it would be on another educational issue that Fr. Titus would intervene more decisively, if that is possible. In August 1941 the government issued a rule that obliged Catholic schools to expel Jewish children, even if they had converted to Catholicism. Brandsma, in his capacity as president of the Catholic schools, sent a circular letter to Catholic schools in which he openly rejected this regulation with firm arguments:

> After having consulted with the competent authority and having taken note of the point of view of the Protestants, I inform you that the forced expulsion from the instruction of the Church of those people who request it, we feel is a flagrant injustice and should be considered as an attack on the mission of the Church itself. The Church, in carrying out its mission, knows no distinction of sex, race, or people. We can distinguish, however, two groups of students among those who request instruction in our Catholic schools. First, the group of students who ask for it as a matter of principle, since, having converted to our faith, they desire Catholic instruction. Then there would be the second group of those who, being non-Catholics, request admission to Catholic schools for only material secondary reasons. As for the first group, we must positively hold the view that we cannot refuse their admission to our colleges. Regarding the second, although there is no obligation in principle for admission, neither are there reasons of principle to reject it. I would like to hear, as soon as possible, to what extent the measures that refer to Jewish students affect your school and what consequences are derived from them ...

This letter must have had some effect, since the regulations from the government were slightly relaxed: those Jewish children who had received Catholic training before May 1940 and could prove it, could remain in Catholic schools. However, shortly thereafter, that easing up was revoked and the regulations were re-instated with their initial harshness. It seems that the regulations were not followed in the two Carmelite colleges, Oldenzaal and Oss, where Brandsma had played a key role in their foundation some years earlier. This also changed with the mass deportation of Jews following the Wannsee conference.

It appears that Sophie Van Berckel, special advisor to the Archbishop on Jewish affairs, greatly assisted Fr. Titus in these very delicate steps. Although, of course, the efforts carried out by both were kept completely secret, we know that they collaborated closely in their defense of the Jews. Titus Brandsma even worked on the possibility of sending Jewish children to Brazil. It is something that could not be documented. But there has always been a rumor that, in the last months before his arrest, they were planning something like this. Both would pay for it with their lives since Sophie Van Berckel was transported and died in Sachsenhausen in 1944. Apparently, Titus also tried to help Jewish children through the Apostolate of Reunification, as is clear from the minutes of the group meeting on November 27, 1941. Undoubtedly, the active professor was aware of the seriousness of the situation and used all possible means to help the persecuted Jews.

5.4. Confrontation by the Press

The second area over which Fr. Titus struggled with the occupation authorities was that of the press. In fact, this would become the precise reason for his arrest. Fr. Titus' true vocation in journalism and the development of the Catholic press in the Netherlands, a predominantly Protestant country, was well known. This explains the virulence of the confrontation.

As we have seen, in 1935 Fr. Titus had been appointed as the ecclesiastical assistant to the Catholic Press by Archbishop Jansens, Archbishop De Jong's predecessor. When the occupation government began to pressure Catholic newspapers to publish Nazi publicity and anti-Semitic slogans, both De Jong and his assistant, Fr. Titus, quickly realized the significance of the situation. A Catholic newspaper could in no way compromise itself with such imposed propaganda. This collided head-on not only with his deepest religious convictions but also with the journalistic ethics he had always defended.

On August 10, 1940, at a meeting of the various press associations held in Utrecht, and from which he left quite disappointed when he saw the lack of unity in the face of the invading force, Fr. Titus presented his resignation to the archbishop. De Jong was able to persuade him to continue in the position. The National Socialist government intensified its pressure on the press, requiring them to publish Nazi material with increasing frequency. But the Dutch episcopate was not intimidated and firmly issued strict communiqués through which Catholics were told clearly that they could not collaborate with the occupying force. Perhaps for this reason, Fr. Titus, with his usual honesty and firm mindset, felt not only supported but also obliged to continue defending the interests of the Catholic Church and its fundamental principles. The culmination came on December 18, 1941 when the Ministry of Propaganda and Arts sent a statement to all the newsrooms of the newspapers which announced:

> It is forbidden to reject for reasons of principle the propaganda that is transmitted to you by National Socialism and its organizations, when it does not contain anything that could damage the honor and well-being of individuals or groups, and does not attack their reputation. And this measure has been taken because we believe that nothing that can promote the unity of the Dutch people should be neglected.

The document, not without a certain cynicism, was not yet official. Father Titus immediately visited Archbishop De

Jong and they decided not to send any public notification from the episcopate but to personally visit the newspaper editors, explaining to them the impossibility of submitting to government blackmail and giving them to understand— with understanding, but with firmness—that, in the case of yielding and publishing the propaganda, the episcopate would withdraw the Catholic status from that publication and would invite the faithful not to buy it. It was a very delicate, difficult and unpleasant mission, since it involved demanding an attitude of almost heroic resistance from the directors. From the moment the Ministry's note came out on December 18, until the arrest of Fr. Titus on January 19, 1942, his activity was frantic and, although his steps were well known by the authorities who were spying on him, Fr. Titus tried to maintain a semblance of normalcy.

On December 31, Fr. Titus wrote to the newspaper editors a letter that would be delivered by hand. It affirmed the Church's acceptance of local and international law but rejected laws imposed against freedom of the press and people's consciences. For this reason, the directors of Catholic newspapers and magazines were again urged not to publish the Nazi propaganda or articles that were officially imposed. The Catholic press assistant ended up acknowledging that it was a tough position, that it would require sacrifices, but that for a believer it was clear and inevitable. God himself—concluded the assistant—would reward the courage of those who serve the word in defense of the faith and of human beings. According to H. W. F. Aukes, one of the first biographers of Saint Titus, this document deserves a place in the annals of the history of the Church.

Curiously, in the midst of this dramatic situation, full of tension, danger, and clandestine activity, Titus Brandsma was also quite active pastorally. We know, for example, that he met with and helped a Protestant society coming from Switzerland, demonstrating again his ecumenical spirit. In the last days before his arrest, he led a retreat of the Third

Order of the Carmelites. Nor did he forget his family in those hectic days. He wrote notes of congratulations on Christmas and the New Year and was interested in his brother Henricus' poor health.

In the first ten days of January Fr. Titus visited fourteen newspapers, four bishops, and ten cities. Some bishops, like Haarlem's, recommended the utmost discretion. Recreating his journey over these days is difficult. Although he traveled openly, he did so with some caution. However, it seems that both knowledge of his travels and a draft of the letter itself were already in the hands of the secret police. During these days a note from the police is sent to Berlin. It includes the name of Brandsma. On January 7, Fr. Titus stopped at the Merkelbeeck convent, where he had lively chats with the Carmelite students and his old friend Fr. Hubert Driessen, who also suggested that he be careful. But the prudent advice of his Carmelite brother and friend was of no avail. Nor was he intimidated by the fact that another professor at the University of Nijmegen, the Jesuit Robert Regout, had been detained for more than a year with no hint of release. In fact, he would be transferred to Dachau, where he would die in December 1942, a few months after Fr. Titus.

Fr. Titus felt strongly encouraged by the reaction of the newspaper editors with whom he was meeting. They showed excellent moral values, despite their distressing situation, and in most cases expressed their unconditional support to Fr. Titus. He could not leave them in the lurch. He could not fail those who followed the Church's directives with such costly fidelity.

At the same time, the Nazi authorities knew of his efforts and were already studying his case. Officer Janke wrote a memorandum, probably based on the betrayal of someone who reported Brandsma, and suggested arresting him. But two sections of the occupying government were competing for "the prey," which probably delayed the arrest by a few days: Section III on the press and Section IV on religious matters in which Hardegen worked, directed by Wolf, and who would finally be in charge of "the Brandsma case."

On January 13, two polite "students" asked at the convent gate for Professor Brandsma, who was not there. On the 14th he received two or three calls from unknown students. The rope was tightening. On January 15, Nazi orders regarding the press were officially confirmed. Archbishop De Jong urgently called Brandsma. The draft of the letter that he had presented to the directors was accepted by the bishops who would assume it as their own. It would be made public immediately. The following day they began to receive accessions from the various newspapers, with a common motto: "*We will resist!*"

In these weeks before the arrest, Fr. Titus showed great energy. It seems to have been a period in which his health agreed to cooperate with him. His spirit seemed quite positive, despite the dire situation of the country, the dark forecasts of the war and the tremendous danger it was facing. He was not unaware of his personal danger and the consequences of his actions. In fact, months before, the Frisian Carmelite had spoken and preached several times about death and even gave a retreat on the theme of "Learning to Die." Perhaps he was preparing himself.

He still had time on January 17 to travel to Oldenzaal where he looked for a family to take care of an orphaned Armenian child. That young victim of the war, as those of all wars, needed a family, a roof, and a dinner plate—and that could not wait. On the 18th, he ate at the Janssen's. Professor Janssen was the professor of Latin on the faculty. On the next day he was in Amsterdam. He celebrated mass in the Church of Saint Boniface (the destiny of both men always seemed to get closer and closer). Then he left for The Hague, where he had to deal with some matters in the education department. The short distance between the Dutch cities allowed him to be in his classroom in Nijmegen by four in the afternoon. Serene and relaxed, he gave what would be his last class. He would, however, give another one—a truly masterful lesson—but in a more existential way. At half past five he arrives at his monastery somewhat tired. He greets the brother porter who tells him that they have asked for him several times. He goes to his room. He has just dropped his wallet and hung up his hat when the convent bell announces a visitor. Again, it is the two, young, neatly dressed men. The brother at the door, with the kindness that Fr. Titus always asked for his visitors, ushers them into a hall. Titus Brandsma hurries downstairs, perhaps aware that a fate awaits him from which he has refused to escape. He is arrested and, after asking a blessing from the prior—someone he would never see again—he is imprisoned that very night.

It was January 19, 1942. The next day, a group of Nazi leaders met in a beautiful villa on the shores of Lake Wannsee, near Berlin. It was a macabre meeting in which the decision would be made to apply the infamous "final solution" (*die Endlösung*) to the so-called "Jewish question" (*die Judenfrage*).

VI

IN THE HORROR OF THE
CONCENTRATION CAMP

6.1. Detention

During the last days of December 1941 and the first days of January 1942, Fr. Titus maintained a truly feverish activity, as we have just seen: visits to newspaper editors, to Archbishop De Jong with whom he maintained close and continuous contact, and his ordinary academic activity—all of this interrupted only by the Christmas holidays and visits to his Carmelite confreres. His movements did not go unnoticed by the German police who followed with great attention.

From this moment on, Professor Brandsma was beginning a personal Way of the Cross. He had entered an impressive police operation. Here he would get to know the bowels of a system that dominated everything and everyone in the name of the State, the race, and order. He would feel within himself the humiliation, the deprivation of all liberty, the purest cruelty. In the months to come he would visit a number of prisons and concentration camps. Throughout this journey, he maintained an astonishing serenity and even an inner joy that surprises those who today read his writings from prison. In these months he writes perhaps the most wonderful pages of his life. As a good journalist, you keep writing until the last moment. Fr. Titus continued to do so until he was deprived of paper, and then he wrote between the lines of another book. Everywhere, he leaves a trace of simplicity and humanity that, many times, surprised even his executioners. It was a warm sign of humanity in the midst of an iron framework, gray and cold, like that month of January 1942 during which Fr. Titus was detained.

But let us return to that detention. The two young men introduced themselves. One was German and his name was Steffen and the other was Dutch. They both belonged to the political police. They announced that he is under arrest and that, after a search of his room, they will immediately leave for Arnhem prison. The community was alerted by the brother porter who understood what was happening. While they begin to go through all the folders and personal papers of Fr. Titus, the porter announced that he had a visitor. It was the editor of the newspaper *De Genderlander* who had come to speak with him. The two agents yelled at the brother to tell all visitors that Fr. Titus was not there. They kept some papers. Fr. Titus collected his personal belongings quickly. In the rush he forgot his rosary. The community gathered at the door of his room. Fr. Titus briefly explained what was happening and emotionally said goodbye to his Carmelite brothers. He tried to seem serene and even joked to the agents that their delay will cause them to miss the train. When he came before the prior, and following custom, he asked his permission to leave the house and for his blessing.

They took the 6:30 train bound for Arnhem. A lady realized what was happening and, with a gesture, indicated that she will pray for him. Several times he tried to converse with his two captors who remain unchanged. Only when faced with a humorous comment by Fr. Titus did one of the two policemen speak and shed a little light on their situation. Fr. Titus commented on his surprise at being arrested after 60 years of honorable life, to which Steffen replied: "*You should not have accepted the order of the archbishop.*" Fr. Titus understood then that these men knew quite a bit about his movements in recent days.

He stayed in Arnhem only that night. The next day he was transferred to Scheveningen prison, on the outskirts of The Hague. Apart from how difficult it was for the Germans to pronounce the prison's name correctly, it was better known as the "Hotel Orange" since there were many prisoners detained there for their loyalty to the Dutch monarchy, the House of Orange. Fr. Titus himself still wore on his lapel the decoration received two years earlier from the hands of Queen Wilhelmina. He thought his stay in prison would be short. He believed, with his usual optimism, that it would be a matter of procedure until the situation was clarified. For this reason, he suggested to the person in charge of the cells that he would surely only be there for a few days, to which the man responded with a certain irony that he—three years earlier—had thought the same thing.

On January 20 Fr. Titus was interrogated for the first time. The case manager was a Sergeant Major Hardegen. He was a curious character: refined in manners, cultured, with a pleasant manner, perhaps somewhat affected. He treated Professor Brandsma with some deference. His questions were subtle, and they were linked together according to the prisoner's answers. Perhaps Hardegen expected a different reaction from the Carmelite, more defensive, more nervous. But Fr. Titus was firm, serene, even friendly. He responded to everything with an honest interest in collaborating. He assumed responsibility for his mission to newspaper editors. He acknowledged that he had been commissioned by the Catholic hierarchy, on whose behalf he was acting, specifically by Archbishop De Jong. But he personally felt completely responsible for the visits. There was a curious relationship between the two, almost a mutual admiration despite the abyss that separated them. It was somewhat similar to that between Jesus of Nazareth and the Roman procurator of Judea some 1,900 years earlier.

This terrible clash between two characters who seem to admire one another, despite defending totally antagonistic conceptions of life and of the human being, was well presented in the RAI film *Le due Croci,* which portrays the last years of Fr. Titus' life. It is directed by Silvio Maestranzi, with performances by Heinz Bennent (as Fr. Titus), Pamela Villoresi, Jacques Breuer, William Berger, and others. In this cinematic fiction, both personalities come across as strong, convinced, and tenacious. They face each other head on but convey some sense of admiration for one another.

Interestingly, Hardegen should not have been in charge of this case. He oversaw Section IV of the police organization, the one dedicated to problems with the churches, and, specifically, Section B concerning the Catholic Church. In a letter dated January 19, addressed to the Security Service, Oscar Vogel, in charge of Section III-A for problems with the confessional press, complained that he was not assigned Professor Brandsma's case. Not even such anonymous and impersonal machinery was capable of nullifying zealots and personal ambitions. The data surpasses the anecdote. Many years later, in the process of beatification, this would be taken into account. In the minds of the Nazis, the crime of Fr. Titus was essentially of a religious nature.

Hardegen understood that he was not dealing with a common detainee. Before him was a man of great spiritual and intellectual stature. It was not easy to undermine either his morale or his arguments. He seemed to fear nothing and to act incredibly naturally. Hardegen had much information about Professor Brandsma's activities, and he used it strategically, as if to imply that the prisoner was really trapped. But Fr. Titus did not lie. He did not need to hide anything. He acknowledged that he had dedicated himself to visiting the newspaper directors, seeking to create a common front against the unfair regulations that had been imposed on them. This common front would act within the law but would publicly show its dissatisfaction. There was nothing to hide. The position of the Catholic hierarchy would, however, be quite firm. Those newspapers that gave in to Nazi pressure would no longer be considered Catholic, and he even cited for Hardegen the example of the *Residentiebode*, which, after being sanctioned by the ecclesiastical authority as a non-Catholic newspaper, found its circulation so diminished that it was forced to close.

Fr. Titus also let the sergeant major know that the vast majority of directors had agreed to resist, despite the great sacrifice being asked of them. The interrogation—of which we retain today the minutes signed by both interlocutors—shows that the issue was complex and that neither Titus nor Hardegen were willing to compromise on their approaches.

Faced with all these responses, Hardegen asked the elderly professor to explain in writing why he and the Dutch Catholics opposed National Socialism. Professor Brandsma had mastered the subject, having preached on it and having devoted many classes to it at the university. That same night Fr. Titus began to write the letter that had been requested of him. Hardegen would not ask him for it until months later. But Fr. Titus went to work on it as if he were trying to prepare another piece for some publication. He pointed out the foreign nature of National Socialism, which could hardly fit in with the character and philosophy of the Dutch, who were naturally calm and peaceful. National Socialism starts from erroneous assumptions, both philosophical (a certain interpretation of Hegel and, above all, of Nietzsche), and sociological (the belief that Europe has fallen into an unacceptable decadence and degeneration caused by democracies and the action of the Jews). Furthermore, the ideological character of Nazism and its bombastic dogmatism collide head-on with the pragmatic realism of the Dutch, who are more prone to seek practical solutions to everyday problems than to wield lofty words without much meaning. For this reason, the NSB members who occupied the key positions of the administration, faced with a significant lack of popular support, became arrogant and inefficient and acted childishly, asking for help from the "older brother"—German Nazism.

Fr. Titus made no bones about it. He even added that the deeply religious Dutch people already had many martyrs, both in the Catholic and Protestant Church, and that they were capable of accepting martyrdom, again in defense of the faith inherited from their elders.

Fr. Titus concluded by showing his respect for international law and for the occupation government—but only as a provisional power which the Dutch would accept while awaiting a solution that would restore their freedom. Not even then did this man lose his greatness of spirit. He thus ended with a blessing, making real the Gospel imperative to pray for those who persecute you (Mt 5: 44). This discussion is also a proof of Fr. Titus' intuition. It was not the German people who were the torturers, but a particular ideology, which, perhaps, had taken root in that people because of certain historical circumstances. They would end up as victims of it as well. Even today we read those final lines of Fr. Titus with emotion, written with shaky handwriting, but still firm:

> God save Holland! God save Germany! May God grant these two peoples to walk again in peace and freedom and recognize his Glory for the good of these two nations so close.

In a way, it reminds us of Etty Hillesum who, in the midst of Nazi persecution, dares to affirm in her letters, "It is a lot of love that I carry inside, towards Germans and Dutch, towards Jews and non-Jews, towards all of humanity." Or of Jesuit Fr. Arrupe and the deep inner freedom he felt when upon entering the Hiroshima prison, accused of having had contacts with spies. Or of so many others who, throughout the centuries and in the most extreme situations, have known how to maintain their deepest inner freedom, the most overwhelming serenity, and the most moving charity—even towards their jailers and executioners. All of them, in those moments when everything invited hatred, made our fundamental Christian vocation come true: to bless! (1 Peter 3: 8-9).

Hardegen sent in his report on the prisoner, who had become prisoner Z-B-78. His report summarizes the case and warns of the risk posed by the detainee, since he tends to undermine National Socialist policies, and thus exerts a negative influence on public opinion. For this reason, the report recommended "preventive detention," a legal device widely used by the SS that allowed them to imprison a person without having to go through the "formalities" of a fair trial. In his report, the Judicial Sergeant stressed that Fr. Titus was a man of character, with very deep convictions, who believed in the obligation to defend Christianity from the attacks of National Socialism. Because he had opposed in writing the National Socialist policy against the Jews and was so open in his overall opposition to Nazism, Fr. Titus had to be considered a dangerous man. At the conclusion of their meeting, Hardegen joked cynically, "It will not be difficult for him to stay in the cell, given his status as a friar." He did not know how accurate this comment was.

Titus Brandsma was assigned to cell 577 of the Scheveningen prison. That small room would have been suffocating for anyone, but Titus paradoxically found there a haven of peace and tranquility. In that small cell he could reflect on one of the most intense experiences of his life, and he would write some beautiful pages that reveal the true dimensions of his spirit. But he never lost sight of the danger to which he was exposed, much less the firmness he had to show in fulfilling his mission. Perhaps in this he was a bit naive. His mission—at least as he had carried it out to that point—was over.

Fr. Titus got down to work. He tried to create a small life plan in that cell and began by organizing his living space. He paid attention to small details. Someone had said that "to adorn is to adore," and the prisoner was making it happen. Perhaps he was also reproducing the attitude of the early Carmelites who first of all, as the Rule of St. Albert instructs, build and prepare a space and organize the time to develop their life of prayer and penance. In other writings, I have highlighted that dimension of our Rule which creates an "oikos," a spiritual home for human growth and encounter with the Lord. Even in these dramatic conditions, the Dutch Carmelite tried to recreate that environment, and a close analysis of his writings from the period suggests that he was successful. In fact, Brandsma regularly referred to his "little cells," perhaps with a desire to create that spiritual *oikos.* Early on, in a letter addressed to his mother from the novitiate for her birthday, he told her how happy he was in his monastic life and gave her a brief description of his cell:

> I am very happy in my cell and with my brothers.... My cell is just a small square room with a window. On one wall is my bed and on the other wall there is a table with a shelf, on which are the statues of Jesus, Mary and Joseph."

Titus placed several images around his cell in Scheveningen. Among them was the poem in Spanish of Saint Teresa: "*Nothing disturbs you, nothing frightens you.*" A quote much loved by Fr. Titus, today it appears on the small monument at the entrance to the house in Ugokloster where he was born. He also had in his breviary an image of Our Lady of Mount Carmel, which he carefully opened and placed in a corner. And he had a picture of Jesus crucified by Fra Angelico. Profoundly moved by it, he wrote *Before a Picture of Jesus in My Cell*. He would give a copy of that poem to a fellow prisoner, and it would eventually find its way around the world.

Fr. Titus also tried to organize his time, making a small schedule. Accustomed as he was to intense activity, it seemed to him that prison left him so much "free" time that he felt the need to organize and work. Imbued with the current spirit of religious life, which in the Dutch province was very pronounced, and by the mentality of the so-called Touraine Reform of the Order that valued a strict observance of schedules, Fr. Titus also organised a timetable, which was really nothing more than a somewhat illusory way of imposing order and rhythm onto the nonsense of his prison life.

6.2. Scheveningen: Letters from Jail

This small effort toward order in the midst of the chaos of prison gave Fr. Titus a chance to write some of the most interesting pages of his career—and it would pay off. First, he wrote *My Hours* and then *My Cell*. Both would later be bound together in the *Diary of a Prisoner*. In them he peels back with simplicity and depth the experience of prison, his feelings, his fears, his devotions, his prayers, and above all, his great trust in God. He often quotes his spiritual teachers and shows a fine sense of humor, even while remaining aware of his grave situation. He describes the little tricks he used to make that icy prison cell in Scheveningen more pleasant. For example, his watch had been confiscated but was later returned. So, he set it without knowing what time it actually was. He jokes about it, "The truth is that my watch works quite well, although without regard to Greenwich Mean Time, Amsterdam or Berlin."

In Scheveningen Fr. Titus "celebrated" his 62nd birthday on February 23, 1942. Like all prisoners, he participated in mandatory gymnastics almost every day. At first—he tells the story himself—the other prisoners looked on in amazement at the old priest dressed in black, who wore the Orange-Nassau insignia on his chest; but later they got used to it. "I don't have much practice in these exercises, but I try to do the best I can ... it's hilarious." Despite Fr. Titus' good humor, we know a lot about those gymnastic sessions, often in the midst of snow. Without even approaching the harshness that lay ahead in the other camps, already in Scheveningen Fr. Titus saw several colleagues collapse—victims of fatigue, malnutrition, and despair. Many of them were professors, writers, and lawyers—almost all of them advanced in years, and not all with the predisposition of Fr. Titus' mindset.

However, what most mortified Fr. Titus about the prison schedule were the long hours—not sleeping, but just staying in bed. The light was always turned off very early in the evening until the next day, perhaps to save electricity. For an active spirit like his, who thrived in his work and his "projects" of tireless creativity, those long hours of inactivity and darkness—those eternal nights of the frozen Dutch winter—were a real ordeal. To top it all, on January 29, the feast of Saint Francis de Sales, patron saint of journalists, his pipe and tobacco were taken away. The young guard who did this insisted that the order had come "from above" and that it was not his fault. Titus understood perfectly, but he would write that he had to remember "the sweet Francis de Sales," to placate himself. He simply deleted the word smoking from his schedule.

In his month and a half in Scheveningen, Fr. Titus wrote two letters—or at least they are all that remain. In them he shows an admirable strength of mind. He is interested in everyone, congratulates his sister on her birthday, asks about students and colleagues. Above all, he tries to reassure both his Carmelite brothers and his relatives, who had hardly heard from him since the day of his arrest. He made efforts to encourage Archbishop De Jong. *"Tell Archbishop De Jong not to worry or blame himself for anything, as I suffer with joy and feel quite well and happy."* When the Archbishop heard the message from the prior of the Carmelites of Nijmegen, he could not help but shudder.

Fr. Titus was also able to begin his oft-postponed *Life of Saint Teresa*. It seems that before the German invasion, he had already arranged its publication with the Spectrum publishing house. Yet several more times, he had delayed the work. Now he was determined to do it. He had with him only *Mystical Doctor* translated by Thomas Kwakman, one of the two books that they allowed him to take, and all the erudition stored up from years of study. He was able to write more than 300 pages. The first are written on regular paper with the letterhead of the prison, including certain regulations regarding prisoner mail and family visits (which, in practice, no longer existed). At some point, it appears that the paper was withdrawn, so he continued to write between the lines of the other book, *A Life of Jesus* by Cyril Verschaeve. This book was recovered after the war and is still preserved as a relic by the Dutch Carmelites. The handwriting, which in the first chapters is clear and firm, gets worse as one turns the pages. The very expression of ideas became difficult, which suggests that Brandsma's condition was not as rosy as he implied in his reassuring letters. In some of the final letters he still asked that they let Fr. Hubert Driessen know that he is working on the Saint Teresa project and that he has already prepared a good part. In addition, he wrote a small *Way of the Cross*, thinking of the land prepared for devotions to Saint Boniface in Dokkum, the exact location of the saint's martyrdom, as we saw above.

The situation seemed to drag on. Days and weeks passed, but a quick release did not come. On March 12, Fr. Titus received a surprise visit from one of the guards, who briefly gave him a ray of hope. He was going to leave Scheveningen, not for freedom but for the Amersfoort concentration camp. From Scheveningen we have his writing from which the spiritual man emerges—a man of depth and inner richness—the mystical experience that Fr. Titus carried within himself and which some had doubted due to his busy life.

On January 27, 1942, Saint Titus concluded his diary with these startling words:

> "Beata solitudo" (blessed solitude). I am in this cell as in my own home. So far, I have not been bored at all, quite the opposite. I am alone, it is true, but the Lord is closer to me than ever. I feel like shouting for joy because the Lord has wanted me to discover him in all his fullness, without needing to be among men, or for men to come here. He is my only refuge. I feel happy. I will always remain here if He wills it. Few times have I felt so happy ...

6.3. Amersfoort

Along with another group of prisoners, crammed into trucks, they left for a place unknown to most of them. Fr. Titus looked out on the fields and the small towns they passed through with a certain nostalgia. Those landscapes viewed from captivity acquired another meaning, as something from every day, wonderful, but now forbidden. In that truck, Fr. Titus began a conversation with several prisoners. An affable and approachable man by nature, he already felt the weeks that he had spent almost incommunicado. The mood, however, was not conducive to much talk. Over those men hung the shadow of a more than uncertain future. Proof of this is the anecdote mentioned earlier: one of the prisoners, Van Mierlo, asked one of the priests to hear his confession. But the priest had certain scruples, not knowing if he was authorized to hear confessions. When Fr. Titus was consulted, he told the priest not to worry and to hear the man's confession without any scruples. Van Mierlo and Fr. Titus developed a great friendship from that moment on.

Arriving at the prison camp while it was still early morning, the prisoners endured all the admissions procedures. Naked, shaved, and numbered like animals, they stood waiting for hours and hours in the snow until they received their new uniforms. Fr. Titus was assigned the number 58. All of this was part of a cruel and depersonalizing process by which the identity of the subject was gradually being cancelled, reducing human beings to a number. They soon met Karl Berg, a brutal man given charge of the SS for their section, and "Nelis," one of the *Kapos* so nicknamed by the prisoners, famous for his inhumane methods. Fortunately, Father Titus found interesting companions during his time in that camp. There were other priests, teachers, artists, intellectuals, and all kinds of citizens who, at one point or another, had committed the irreparable blunder of standing up to the occupation government.

Another Carmelite on the way to her martyrdom, would also pass through the same Amersfoort prison a few months later. Edith Stein, after educating herself in the Jewish faith of her family and after long years of philosophical research as one of the best students of Edmund Husserl, had converted to Christianity and professed vows in Carmel. Due to her Jewish origins, she had to leave her native land of Germany and seclude herself in a Dutch convent, where she would be arrested. In early August of that same year, she would pass through Amersfoort on her way to some extermination camp in Germany. Finally, she would be sent to Auschwitz in Poland, where she was killed on August 9.

The "transit" camp (or *Durchgangslager*) of Amersfoort was closely connected to another, Westerbork, and convoys frequently came and went in both directions. Etty Hillesum, another passionate figure, tells us in her letters of that exchange at Amersfoort. Her diary ends with the thought that she would try to be a balm for so many wounds, an overwhelming commitment that Fr. Titus also seemed to take on. Within those two connected camps, we find three of the most sublime figures in the spiritual history of the last century.

In Amersfoort the prisoners shared their skills. One made a small crown with branches, from which he hung a wooden cross. This is kept today by Fr. Titus' nieces and nephews as a relic. Another man manufactured a small rosary with buttons for "Uncle Titus," as he began to be called. That rosary would accompany him until the moment of his death and would be his last gift. John Dons, another companion in misfortune, drew Fr. Titus in his prison uniform. Dons was a good artist, especially of landscapes but he was able to capture the fatigue and vulnerability of his fellow inmate. In the sketch, next to the number 58, is a red triangle to identify political prisoners and differentiate them from Jews who wore a yellow star or from Dutch army officers who wore a green one. Some weeks later, John Dons would be shot; but before he died, he asked to be allowed to paint a landscape, which was granted to him. It was a typical Dutch landscape with a river, fields of colored flowers that evoke the Dutch flag, a typical church in the background, and a somewhat cloudy sky. Certainly, this final painting is a powerful testament to beauty in a place as seedy as the Amersfoort concentration camp.

The prisoners looked for any pretext to mentally escape from that suffocating atmosphere. One of Fr. Titus' fellow inmates tells how one day they had fun puzzling out different meanings for the acronym *P.D.A.* for *Polizeiliches Durchgangslager Amersfoort* (Amersfoort Police Transit Camp). These letters were everywhere in the camp. Fr. Titus suggested turning them into *Probamur dum amamur* (We are tested, because we are loved). He made friends with a Protestant pastor and with J. Aalders, a diocesan priest in whose parish he had preached some years before. The testimony of Aalders, as well as that of other fellow prisoners, will helpfully illuminate what happened in those weeks.

Those who lived with him in these moments certify how Fr. Titus maintained his affable and open character, despite the fact that Amersfoort far surpassed Scheveningen in difficulty. The end of the Dutch winter was very cold that year. On many mornings they only had roll call after enduring many hours in the snow. Hunger was the great invisible presence in the camp. Inmates sometimes fought over a crust of bread and took turns to scrape the large pots from which the simple food was served. Fr. Titus, like all the others, would approach when it was his turn to pick up the remaining bits of food with his fingers. Van Mierlo, who had been with him since their conversation in the truck to Amersfoort, talked about how despite the sadness of the situation—swinging from the grotesque to the tragic—Brandsma did not lose his serenity. It was bitterly sad to see these men foraging for scraps of food, fighting starvation.

In the labor camp, Fr. Titus was assigned to the lumberjack group. They soon realized his weakness, which made him useless for the job. He was then sent to the group in charge of peeling potatoes. He writes in a letter that this work allowed him to pray with his mind and heart while he helped his companions with his hands. At dusk the prisoners returned for review. Tired, freezing to death, some like living ghosts, they responded blandly when they heard their name. Dysentery took its toll on the prisoners. The camp authorities were forced to set up one of the barracks as an infirmary. When night fell, one of the most ghoulish sounds in the countryside would begin. It was the Russians, prisoners of the Third Reich from the campaign against the Soviet Army. After moving from prison camp to prison camp, they ended up in Amersfoort where they were left on their own until they died from the cold and hunger. Many nights they sang old songs from their homeland, while letting themselves freeze to death, not wanting to enter the prison barracks. This, in turn, displeased the Jews, who were responsible for burying them and preparing the mass graves—a daunting, macabre and absurd spectacle.

But Fr. Titus could not remain inactive for long. In

the barracks they formed a group that would come to be known as "the Tilburg circle." This was a group of believers with some initiative who decided to do something within the very narrow limits imposed by the camp regulations. Sometimes they had small meetings in the rare free time. Fr. Titus spoke to them about a topic in Christian life, especially those related to hope and faith. Some Sundays they celebrated a *sui generis* mass, which included a handshake as a spiritual communion. The survivors of the Tilburg circle would always remember those moments of faith and solidarity.

In the April 21 roll call, to the shout of "Anno Sjoerd Brandsma," no one responded. Among the inmates a rumor spread. "It is Uncle Titus!" With a mixture of pain and anger, some believed that he had been eliminated, probably in one of the savage beatings that were more and more frequent. But it was not that. Fr. Titus had gone to the infirmary because he could hardly stand. Any bit of care or rest, no matter how small, was a relief for a body so weakened. And Titus did feel some slight improvement. Also, the infirmary gave him a magnificent opportunity to work as a priest. He anointed the sick and helped many prisoners die well. He even gained the trust of some of the guards and nurses. This would allow him, upon discharge, to continue visiting the sick, for which he was very grateful. He gave special care to a young man who was slowly dying in that Hell. He would heat stones in the stove and would use them, carefully wrapped, to warm the beds of the sick. His witness did not go unnoticed. Years later, the few who survived would speak of the deep impression made on them by that small man. "The kindest man in the country," is how one of the witnesses put it. Titus Brandsma, the Carmelite, the university professor, the prisoner, committed himself to that ideal of great and noble souls, which Etty Hillesum once again described so beautifully, "not to add to this depraved world one more drop of hate."

Given the number of intellectuals, doctors, writers, and university professors who were in the camp, they were allowed to organize conferences on various topics. These conferences in the concentration camps were not at all unusual, especially where intellectuals met. We know this from the testimonies in later publications of Etty Hillesum, Jorge Semprún, Petr Ginz and others. Ginz even edited a small magazine in the concentration camp of *Terezin* or *Theresienstadt* near Prague, CZ, and he maintained interesting contacts with intellectuals and writers there. Also in Terezin, Viktor Frankl came to have a psychological consultation service, from which he would gain so much insight for his famous "logotherapy."

Of course, the censorship of these conferences was fierce. In the case of Amersfoort, the speakers were expected to exalt Dutch culture as part of Germanic culture, which had only accidentally been contaminated by Christians, Jews, and Communists. Fr. Titus, just out of the infirmary, was asked to direct the conference on Good Friday. He and the organizers thought of talking about the Dutch mystic Geert de Groote. A conference on de Groote could pass as a literary topic. And Professor Brandsma was well prepared since he had given a lecture on October 16, 1940, the occasion of the sixth centenary of the Dutch mystic's birth in Deventer where de Groote had been born in 1340. Even earlier he had published a series of popular articles on this author in the newspaper *De Gelderlander*. It is likely that on the occasion of the centenary, Fr. Titus would have dedicated several classes to study de Groote's life and thought.

These were especially hard days. The tension in the camp was palpable. Beatings were repeated more frequently, and it was not uncommon to see a man die for any small infraction. Or even worse, he would be left where he fell after a beating so that his public agony would further impress the other prisoners. The prisoners' spirits were as low as they could go. These men lived with a mixture of anger, discouragement, and bitterness.

In his work *Priestblock 25487*, Jean Bernard reports that Christian holidays were especially dangerous dates for priests in the world of the concentration camp. Just a year prior on Good Friday in 1941, several priests had been brutally punished by "the stick," which left them with terrible lasting effects or killed them. In those days there was always a certain fear of retribution, from either the SS or some deeply anti-Christian *Kapos*.

On Good Friday of 1942 the conference on de Groote took place. Several witnesses who survived gave accounts of it. The whole scene was nothing more than a parody, a cruel mockery, in which a small, frail man helped up onto a grimy box under a light as dim as their lives, was going to begin his "conference." An introduction was made by Grunning. Contrary to the norms, the gathering included some bold prisoners from other barracks who, given the fame of "Uncle Titus," had come to listen to him. The professor, as if in the classroom, solemnly took out the script that he had prepared on an old paper. The audience was very diverse: doctors, university professors, royalists, trade unionists, Jews, Communists, Protestants, some common prisoners, and even "the exegetes," visionary types who, Bible in hand, announced the imminent fall of the Führer since he was "the anti-Christ." A few years earlier, the Protestant pastor Martin Niemöller, in a statement sometimes attributed to Bertolt Brecht, had listed them as being prophetic. All came together under the most miserable of conditions, a situation in which the best human being, stripped of everything, seems even more pathetic. Titus understood it perfectly. He felt the harmony that is transmitted from heart to heart, that overflows in the sweaty palms of his hands and that produces a strange sensation in his stomach.

He began with an overview of the mystical literature in the Netherlands, the main authors, the works; but little by little his voice was gaining confidence. Sweaty behind steamed up glasses, a grotesque show full of inner strength conveyed hope on that Good Friday. On a day like this, Jesus—also martyred, humiliated, tortured—stood in solidarity with all people. They were not alone. Christ, God incarnate, shared with them his passion. Among the most miserable of them, in that corner where barbarism had done its worst, there God continued to speak a word of hope to human beings. It was another Good Friday, another Way of the Cross, the eternal Stations of the Cross for a man, for so many people. But the passion of Christ led to the resurrection. For that reason, these captives had to maintain hope and not collapse. Fr. Titus ended with yet another interpretation of that macabre acronym, PDA: *Perseveramur, Deo Adiuvante* (We will resist with the help of God).

His voice was cut short. The silence was intense and excited. Nobody wanted to break that moment. There was some unpleasant comment, but no one responded and in silence they left their seats and moved toward their bunks and the other barracks. Something had changed in Amersfoort. Titus Brandsma, who had never preached well—who had been told by his teachers that he was barely "oratorical" and had a somewhat monotonous voice—had delivered the sermon of his life. He had little left to add other than his life itself.

In the following days many prisoners wanted to confess to him. He helped them as much as he could. They even offered him another lecture, with whatever excuse for the material, but Titus was already dead tired. His trembling words would not retrieve the force of the previous lecture, and he could hardly finish explaining some ideas. It was his Good Friday. Indeed, in the camp it was rumored that he would be released, but he had no illusions. He knew it would be impossible without giving up his most basic principles and betraying the truth. He was unwilling to do that, as he made known to several nearby prisoners. In addition, word of Friday's conference was "leaked" to the *Kapos* in the camp, and a harsh announcement came that the conference would not be allowed.

On April 22 Fr. Titus learned of his transfer back to Scheveningen to undergo further interrogation. The most optimistic encouraged him, "Surely freedom is near." But Fr. Titus sensed that it was not. This period of darkness, doubts, and fear brings us closer to the figure of Titus Brandsma. He was neither a hero, nor a suicidal fanatic. Despite his natural optimism, he was aware of the terrible reality that surrounded him and of the future that, in all probability, awaited him. He felt tired, weak, and sick. He sensed that the doors were closing and that only the one that leads to martyrdom remained open. He was afraid and had failed. The testimony of another prisoner, Van de Mortel, who lived with him during these days, is significant in this regard: "Although Titus tried to hide it, sometimes he was very sad, not because of himself, but because he saw how cruel human beings could become towards each other."

Amersfoort's environment was much less conducive to writing than that of Scheveningen where he had been alone in a cell and had more time. Yet despite his increasingly aggravated physical and psychological deterioration, in Amersfoort Fr. Titus wrote a second poem—much less well known than the one he wrote in Scheveningen, it expressed a contemplative resolution and acceptance. It is worth knowing:

> Grief would come and lay me low,
> no chance to make it go away,
> nor with any tears allay,
> else had I done long ago.
>
> Then it came and on me weighed,
> till I lay still and no more wept,
> learned to watch and patience kept;

thereafter it no longer stayed.

All that is passed and set aside;
from far away I still recall
and cannot understand at all
that ancient grief nor why I cried ...

On a rainy April morning he left Amersfoort. From a distance, he said goodbye with a gesture and a blessing for his friend Van Mierlo, who years later would say, "He gave us the most beautiful things for all of us and for the countryside. He left us his blessing."

6.4. Scheveningen Again. Kleve

On April 28, Titus Brandsma returned to the Hotel Orange in Scheveningen. It was already night. He was literally thrown into a dark cell already occupied by two others. They made their introductions in the dark: two young Protestants named Cornelius de Graaft and William Oostdijk. They were both pleasantly surprised to learn that their new cellmate was the famous Professor Brandsma from the University of Nijmegen. Brandsma acknowledged that, despite missing the solitude of cell 577 from his previous stay in Scheveningen and these present cramped quarters, he was very happy to have their company. The next day the two young men would discover that this Professor Brandsma had little to do with the one they knew from the press: aged, head shaved, wearing a suit that, due to the sparce food in the camps, was a ridiculously excessively large suit—a man much diminished by the rough conditions at the camps. The three soon formed a small community, sharing long conversations with the elderly professor and journalist. He told them about his projects, his travels, and studies. While the two played cards, Fr. Titus prayed off in a corner. Sometimes they even managed to celebrate the Word in an example of real ecumenism. According to the two cellmates, Fr. Titus was extremely deferential and friendly. He asked permission for everything and appreciated any small thing. At night he was very concerned that his cough kept his companions from sleeping. They would also share the news of his tragic fate.

Hardegen again. On May 6, Fr. Titus appeared once more for interrogation by the arrogant sergeant major who, despite his harshness and coldness, was also struck by changes in the prisoner since their previous encounter (*Ecce Homo*). Hardegen took a different approach this time. His questions hardly touched on the subject of the press. Perhaps, over the intervening months, Hardegen had carefully studied all of the Brandsma material and may even have received new information through sources unknown to us. He focused on the Hebrew children—some compromising letters that the two Gestapo agents had found in their room and testimonies about their classes on National Socialism. All of this came up in the new interrogation. An issue that the old Carmelite had forgotten resurfaced in a rather unpleasant way. Hardegen accused Titus of having refused to allow Professor Baader to become *Rector Magnificus* because he was German. In his defense, Fr. Titus reminded him that he also had refused to select a French applicant because he wanted to keep the University free from national rivalries. But there was much against Fr. Titus. His decisive action in favor of freedom of the press and of teaching seemed clear and, therefore, opposed to the German project in the Netherlands.

According to the interrogation, Fr. Titus could only have been saved by "correcting" his opinions and publicly declaring the good intentions of Nazism in power. But he would not consider that a possibility. Hardegen himself invited Fr. Titus to pick up the phone and notify his Carmelite superiors of his immediate departure for Dachau, the concentration camp near Munich in Bavaria. The conversation—almost a monologue—was short-lived. In a broken voice—it had been several months since he had spoken to those closest to him—Fr. Titus indicated to the prior, Fr. Christopher Verhallen, that he was being interrogated in The Hague and that he would be leaving for Dachau, one of the largest concentration camps in Germany. This transfer would almost certainly guarantee his internment until the end of the war. He tried to cheer up his Carmelite brothers saying "I am fine. I think I will be able to resist." But at the insistence of Hardegen, who was about to interrupt the conversation, Titus quickly said goodbye. "I cannot speak anymore. Goodbye." The efforts of the Carmelite prior, who would remember this conversation with emotion for many years, were useless.

That same night his two cellmates also learned of their friend's fate. They tried to encourage him. Fr. Titus himself seemed to have accepted the news. But he knew that his fate, coupled with that fateful destination in Bavaria, was quite dark. Yet, he still had the courage to write to his family. It was almost as if he were on vacation, sending notes to friends, acquaintances, students, and his brothers in community. A phrase from that letter, written in handwriting that is not recognizable as his, says much about the prisoner's personality:

> Although I am back in Scheveningen, it is just for a short period. They have decided to send me to the Dachau camp, near Munich and I will go there soon, probably next Saturday. I will also find friends there and God is everywhere.

In the few days before leaving, he still had the opportunity to establish a relationship with one of his jailers, an Austrian named Kirzig. He had long conversations with the elderly priest and, some witnesses believe, went to confession to him. But Brandsma's departure was indeed near. On May 16 he left for Dachau. He said goodbye to his two young friends. They all sensed that this was a final farewell. But still that abused little man kept a certain dignity, as one who is heading towards his fate with a firm step and the inner peace of one who had fulfilled his mission.

Again the trucks arrived and the prisoners crowded together. There were hours of waiting for no apparent reason. The wheels of Nazi machinery continued inexorably, devastating lives and consciences. And again, there was a prisoner train. Probably as Edith Stein had in Breslau and Victor Frankl had in Vienna, Titus Brandsma passed through his own town of Nijmegen on the rails that took him to the German border, from Scheveningen to Kleve. It is difficult to imagine what incredble nostalgia they would have felt on viewing from the windows of a prison train, under the most inhumane conditions, their own cities—the cities in which they had lived, worked, and loved.

The road ended sooner than planned. The prisoners arrived at Kleve, a "transit camp" (*Durchgangslager*) for prisoners arriving from and departing to various other points. That camp offered a relative sanity in contrast to the collective hysterias and absurdities that Fr. Titus had been living among for several months. Ultimately though, like everything else, it depended on the Gestapo and the Party. Kleve was still being run by the old German judicial authorities, who had retained a certain sense of legal correctness. Even among those in charge, there were those who would show their disagreement with the prevailing ideology. All of this translated into relatively more humane treatment and a somewhat more relaxed atmosphere.

Fr. Titus initially occupied cell 69 but quickly moved to cell 27, where he once again lived in misfortune with two companions. One of them was an Italian non-commissioned officer, who constantly recalled his country and lamented his bad luck and the habitual hunger to which all prisoners were subjected. Fr. Titus more than once laughed heartily at the man's witticisms. Sometimes he shared part of his food with the Italian; and this, on one occasion, would cost him dearly upon discovery by one of the guards who reprimanded them severely. The other cellmate was a Protestant pastor, Kaptein, a deep man who quickly attached himself to the Carmelite and spoke with him on many different topics. Together they managed to create a somewhat more humane and familiar environment in the midst of that inhuman situation. Fr. Titus "decorated" the cell with a paper cross, but it was seen and thrown away by one of the guards—much to the annoyance of the Italian prisoner whom Fr. Titus frequently consoled.

Attitudes toward religion were much more open at Kleve. Fr. Titus received an old black cassock and a missal. He met the camp chaplain, Ludwig Deimel, who would become a great friend. He left some spiritual books for Titus' enjoyment, but it seems that he had already lost his concentration and was displaying a very noticeable fatigue. The chaplain sometimes brought sweets made by his own mother, hoping to supplement the very poor camp diet. On Sundays mass was offered in the Catholic chapel. It was sung with the accompaniment of a small harmonium, and the prisoners were even able to receive communion. All of this seemed wonderful to Fr. Titus. And the chaplain had permission to freely enter the cells to hear the confessions of prisoners. This allowed him to chat with them and offer a little encouragement. Such moments of support by some of those who worked in this type of institution were not uncommon, as became known after the war.

Titus Brandsma was himself again. Even the chaplain, determined to help him, spoke to him about the possibility of finding a solution. Perhaps clemency could be sought based on the his health. But an initiative like that would have to come from the Carmelites of Nijmegen, that is, from his own superiors. Deimel the chaplain went to work. To prevent the message from being intercepted, he used a system of pure espionage. Taking advantage of an iron exporter who frequently traveled the Nijmegen-Kleve route and could cross the border with relative ease, the chaplain sent a small note typed on very light paper and tucked into the bottom of a tobacco packet. If discovered, Deimel would have paid with his life for such a crime.

Had the initiative been successful, it would not have been the first case of a prisoner who was allowed to move from the camps to house arrest. However, it was not very common—and much less so as the war progressed. The Germans did not want many witnesses coming out of those wicked places which in a few years would become notorious—to humanity's collective shame.

Jan Van Herik, who was the intermediary, arrived in Nijmegen. With all possible discretion he approached the Carmelite convent at the address provided by Deimel. He was greeted at the door, but no one invited him in. The superior told him that they would discuss the case, and he was dismissed without further ado. Van Herik was surprised by the coldness of Titus' companions. But it was clear. They feared that he was a fake intermediary, seeking evidence against the Carmelites of that city or even against Titus himself. It was common for secret Gestapo policemen to infiltrate the ranks of the resistance, which often resulted in harsh reprisals, even against relatives. In addition, the Carmelites—like Fr. Titus' family—did not know where their brother, Titus, was. Perhaps they thought he was already in Dachau. But when a second message arrived—and then a third—the Carmelites began to think that they were dealing with a true collaborator. The plan was to convince Hardegen that Fr. Titus could serve his unspecified sentence while being held in a convent in Germany; he would report regularly to the Gestapo from there. The names of Straubing, Mainz and, above all, Bamberg, in Bavaria were suggested. Even the Carmelite convent of Vienna was discussed. All of them were well-known to Fr. Titus from his time of doctoral studies in Rome. He had used the summers to travel to Bavaria, learn German, and help with ministry in some of the Carmelite houses. He had also spent much time in Vienna while recovering from one of his health crises and preparing for a second attempt at his doctoral exams.

The prior of Nijmegen then turned to a lawyer who was Fr. Titus' second cousin, Asuerus Brandsma, who advised the prior of Bamberg about the possibility of transferring Fr. Titus there. But the mission failed. Hardegen pointed out that the detainee's illness was no excuse since he should have taken that illness into account before undertaking his subversive work. In addition, noted Hardegen, Dachau would attend to the needs of the sick; it was a suitable place for his healing. But there was another matter that Hardegen did not hide, and which helps us to better understand the martyrdom of Fr. Titus. At no time in the process had Titus retracted his opinions about National Socialism or of the deportation of Jews, or of the Nazi influence on the press. For this reason, it was likely that once he was released, instead of showing his gratitude to the Third Reich, he would continue as others had before. After being released, he would return to subversion and sabotage. Professor Brandsma should serve his punishment in prison.

At Kleve, meanwhile, Fr. Titus had written a letter to the prior of Nijmegen insisting (as in the secret message sent through Van Herik) on the possibility of exchanging the camp for house arrest in Germany. However, from the style of the letter, it is clear that Titus himself was not very sure of the result of those efforts. As Chaplain Deimel would later point out, he encouraged him to keep trying, but Fr. Titus seemed resigned to his end at Dachau. This explains why the refusal of clemency by the Nazi authorities was received with such serenity by Fr. Titus, who only repeated, "We are in God's hands. We are in good hands." In the same letter to the Carmelite superior in Nijmegen, after explaining the possible steps to take, he insisted that although he approves of the idea, he leaves it in his superior's hands. He would write yet another letter from Kleve, which we alluded to earlier. This was to his Franciscan brother Henricus on the occasion of his sixtieth birthday. It is a fine letter, full of a certain nostalgia for the years gone by, but with a deep sense of resignation and, above all, of gratitude. Some paragraphs are worth reproducing:

> Dear Henricus: For your sixtieth birthday, which coincides with the joyous day of *Corpus Christi*, I want to extend my warmest congratulations, as well as my prayer before the Lord, so that he may grant you still many beautiful years of priestly life in your Order. During the week I must settle for a spiritual communion, since here Mass is celebrated only on Sundays (...). Every Saturday about 40 people leave from here for the interior of Germany. This week was not yet my turn, maybe it will be the next. But, a week earlier or later does not matter. I wait quietly (...).

> Who would have thought that for your sixtieth birthday I would congratulate you from a German prison? In these sixty years many beautiful things have happened and now, in this sad time, those past times are remembered with pleasure and satisfaction. But those times will return and we hope it will be soon.

> They are still trying to have me under house arrest in one of our houses in Germany, as the parish priest Bulters was allowed, with the obligation to remain in Verray. But it seems difficult that this will ever be achieved. I have put everything in the hands of Saint Joseph, who took the Virgin and little Jesus from Egypt to Nazareth. Like Jesus and the Virgin, I entrust myself to his intercession. Join my prayers too.

> Under the circumstances, I am pretty good. I am hanging in there and I think I will get out of this one and then make up for lost time. My transfer to Dachau means seclusion until the end of the war. Here they are gentle and kind to me, but it is always a prison....

Therefore, cheerfully celebrate your sixtieth birthday.
Start it with joy, that I also participate in it.

Deimel, the camp chaplain who was very concerned about the fate of Fr. Titus, also tried directly to have him released to a German Carmelite convent. To do this, he had Fr. Titus seen by a doctor from Cologne, who certified the condition of the patient. With this, he asked Fr. Titus to fill out a letter to the authorities requesting a measure of grace. In this letter he alludes to his state of health, the various stomach bleeds that he had suffered, certain hallucinations, insurmountable fatigue, his general weakness, and insomnia. All of this had been carefully avoided in letters to his family and his companions in Nijmegen. Fr. Titus shakily signed the statement on June 12.

The letter had not yet left the camp post when the direct transfer order to Dachau arrived. Fr. Titus accepted it very calmly, but the chaplain did not. He had invested much hope and effort into the cause. Any further attempt was now impossible. The German priest had been fascinated by the Carmelite's character, especially his simplicity combined with an exquisite intelligence, qualities difficult to maintain under those circumstances. They had had long conversations on very diverse subjects, and in them he had sensed an exceptional personality, a Christian convinced of his mission, who fulfilled it without a hint of self-importance.

On June 13, early in the morning, Fr. Titus Brandsma left Kleve. Fr. Ludwig Deimel was there to say goodbye to his friend, who seemed serene. He was going to travel with a large group of prisoners, all with the same destination. The line of prisoners, chained in pairs, passed by the chaplain who approached them to say goodbye, confident that he would not be reprimanded by the guards. Fr. Titus whispered to him absentmindedly, "Goodbye, dear friend. Nothing bad is going to happen to me. The Lord is with me." They traveled by train, crammed into animal cargo wagons. As they left, Fr. Titus smiled at the man who had helped him so much during his stay in the camp. Fr. Deimel then found tears in his eyes as that shipment left—human beings, reduced to this degradation, a stinking trainload. At the same time, it was a tabernacle where, better than anywhere else, the suffering Christ could be glimpsed. Deimel could not help but cross himself.

6.5. And Dachau

On June 19, 1942, Professor Brandsma entered the Dachau concentration camp. This was the first concentration camp that had been built in 1933 by the Nazi authorities. It was located in the small town of the same name, Dachau, famous for its school of landscape painting. The camp had been built on the grounds of a former gunpowder factory, closed in accordance with the Treaty of Versailles after the First World War. From March 1933 to April 1941, more than 40,000 prisoners passed through the camp, and many would die there. More than 2,700 priests, religious and even some bishops were imprisoned in the camp. It is estimated that about 1,000 died there.

Fr. Titus probably passed through the iron gate on which the inscription *Arbeit macht frei* ("Work Makes One Free") can be read. The welcome ritual proceeded: general shaving, hours of standing, showers with liquid acid soap for disinfection, humiliations, photographs, footprints, delivery of the prison uniform and clogs, learning songs and slogans. He was assigned barrack 28, one of two barracks dedicated to the hundreds of religious and priests held in the camp.

According to Aukes, Titus also endured a terrible jest that related his Catholicism to the crematoriums: "As you are Catholics, you will celebrate the Ascension in one of the chimneys." The macabre expression recalls other horrific anecdotes of concentration camp literature. For example, psychologist Viktor Frankl reports in *Man's Search for Meaning* that, after going through the initial admission formalities of the camp, he naively asked a colleague about a friend:

> "Was he sent to the left side?"
>
> "Yes," I replied.
>
> "Then you can see him there," I was told.
>
> "Where?" A hand pointed to the chimney a few hundred yards off, which was sending a column of flame up into the grey sky of Poland. It dissolved into a sinister cloud of smoke.
>
> "That's where your friend is, floating up to Heaven," was the answer. But I still did not understand until the truth was explained to me in plain words.

Smoke from chimneys, with the sickly sweet smell of death and annihilation, is a recurring theme in concentration camp accounts. It is neither a literary device nor a metaphor, but the terrible reality. Elie Wiesel, in his famous work *Night*, pointed out that in Auschwitz the cemeteries were high up because the smoke from the chimneys took everything to heaven.

Brandsma received the number 30492. Shortly after entering the camp, he met more fellow prisoners, including some Jesuits belonging to an anti-Nazi group called *Der Deutsche Weg*. He also learned, with no little joy, of the presence in the camp of Brother Raphael Tijhuis, a Dutch Carmelite of his own province. He had been arrested at his residence in Mainz for having sent a letter without return address in which he bemoaned the price of some items in Germany. Brother Raphael's published journal of prison life offers an important testimony of the last days of Fr. Titus and says much about the conditions in that horrible place. He became Professor Brandsma's guardian angel, watching over the old Carmelite, who was ever more tired, weak, and sick. Tijhuis recalls Fr. Titus's capacity for hope, his unshakeable trust in God, his simple and friendly ways with others, his elegant manners—even in that place of absolute human degradation.

Several Polish Carmelites who had been arrested for various reasons were also there. Among them was Fr. Hilary Januszewski, prior of the Carmelite convent in Krakow, the Shrine of Our Lady of the Sands. When the Germans invaded Poland, they strictly prohibited preaching in the Polish language, given the religious fervor of the Polish people and the intense relationship between Catholicism and patriotism that existed there. A Carmelite disobeyed and German soldiers appeared at the monastery to arrest him. But Fr. Hilary incriminated himself, since he was the prior and, thus, the person responsible for everything that happened in the house. This cost him several years in various jails and, finally, in Dachau for several years until he died heroically in 1945, barely a month before the famous *Befreiung*, the liberation of the camp.

A typhus epidemic had broken out in the camp, killing many prisoners. In fact, the *Kapos* remodeled a block as an infirmary, though in reality it was (the prisoner's nickname for it) a "coffin." On one occasion, a *Kapo* taunted the priests and religious, saying that they should talk less about love and go and take care of the typhus patients, which would mean certain death. Everyone stared at the ground. This was just one more cruelty among the many they suffered continuously. Then Hilary Januszewski, a rather quiet man, volunteered for only the second time in his life, and despite the attempt by some Polish priests to restrain him, he went with the *Kapo* to the infirmary block. The proximity of American troops was already rumored in the camp, but Fr. Januszewski would not experience that liberation. He would die at the end of March 1945 infected with typhus. In 1999 he was beatified along with a large group of Polish priests and religious prisoners of Dachau.

The relationship between Titus Brandsma and the

Polish Carmelites over his few weeks in Dachau deserves a more detailed study than we can offer here. We know something of this from the correspondence of Fr. Adrian Staring, vice-postulator for the cause of beatification of Fr. Titus, with Albert Urbański, the Polish Carmelite who wrote a study of clergy in the Dachau concentration camp. In 1955 Staring wrote to the Polish Carmelite asking him why he had mentioned Fr. Titus so little in his work and asking him, if possible, to share some memories he had of the "Servant of God." Fr. Urbański responded very kindly by pointing out how the image of Fr. Titus, always kind and even smiling, had been etched in his memory. He also shared a poignant memory that, two of the Poles having already died when Fr. Titus arrived in Dachau, the Carmelites imprisoned in the camp used to gather discreetly to pray the *Flos Carmeli* together.

In the camp Fr. Titus would also connect with other exemplary priests, such as Fr. Josef Kentenich, the founder of Schonstatt, and other important figures of the Church at that time, mainly German and Polish. One surprising and beautiful fact from Dachau is that, after a series of secret efforts, deacon Karl Leisner, very ill with tuberculosis, was ordained in 1944 by fellow prisoner Bishop Gabriel Piguet, bishop of Clermont-Ferrand. Leisner died in Munich on August 12, 1945, a few months after the liberation of Dachau. He was beatified by John Paul II in 1996. As an aside, we note that the few rudimentary "commemorative cards" of his ordination were drawn by Carmelite Brother Raphael Tijhuis.

As is well known, the camp authorities had built a rudimentary chapel for the clerics who, coming from other camps and prisons, were to be regrouped in this camp near Munich. Use of the chapel varied constantly according to the circumstances of the war or international relations. Thus, when on any level the Church resisted Nazism, the use of the chapel would be restricted. The perverse use that many of the guards made of the supposed "privileges" that the priests had during certain periods of those years in prison is also well-known.

It may also seem surprising that an intense Eucharistic devotion was to be found at Dachau. Some of the priests who were allowed to participate in the Eucharist in the morning—usually only the Germans—would secretly remove a host that would later be divided into tiny particles, thus allowing other priests to receive the sacrament.

Fr. Titus lived in a very profound way during the months in which the Eucharistic devotion passed from one prison to another—at times in the form of nostalgia for its absence. Early in his captivity, from January 20 to March 12, 1942, in *My Schedule, composed* at Scheveningen prison, Brandsma says:

> Afterwards, and always in pajamas that I fortunately took on the day of my arrest, I kneel on the blankets placed on the mat and I celebrate the "mass." I make a spiritual communion, obviously, and a thanksgiving. The celebration is shorter and very different from that of the monastery!

In his *Diary* he wrote, "I certainly miss communion and Holy Mass, but God is close to me, in me, and with me: "*In eo enim vivimur, movemur et sumus.*"

> After spending almost two months without receiving Communion, he was finally able to do so in the transit camp of Kleve before leaving for Dachau. This was a great spiritual consolation for the Carmelite. His friend there, Chaplain Deimel, had tried to get permission for Fr. Titus to celebrate the Eucharist in the prison chapel, but it was not possible.

At Dachau Fr. Titus was able to receive communion from time to time, sometimes with a tiny particle that was passed to him secretly by imprisoned German priests.

Sometimes he divided it further and kept a part. On more than one occasion when he was beaten, he told Brother Raphael, "Don't worry about me, I know who I have by my side. Let's sing the *Adoro Te* (I Adore You). It is not difficult to imagine the consolation that those clandestine communions brought to the Carmelite who was already quite ill and physically exhausted.

But the living conditions of the Dachau camp were too harsh for the fragile health of Fr. Titus, already deteriorated by age and months in prison. On more than one occasion he was savagely beaten by the fearsome *Kapos* for some ommission or some neglect of the rigid discipline of the camp. Despite Brother Raphael's care, Fr. Titus was visibly deteriorating. Food was very scarce; the badly healed wounds on his feet, caused by long walks to workplaces in clogs, brought on a fever. Those closest to him asked him to go to the infirmary. It seems that even Becker, one of the *Kapos*, who had always treated him very badly and who had beaten him on several occasions, was touched and politely asked him to go to the infirmary. Jean Bernard was a priest from Luxembourg and the author of *Pfarrerblock 25487* on which Volker Schlöndorff based his film *Der neunte Tag*. He wrote that the prisoners felt great terror when they were urged to go to the *Revier* or infirmary. They tried by any means to hide or to pretend they were in good health. Fr. Titus also resisted, but ultimately, he gave in. Brother Raphael walked with him as far as he was allowed. He said goodbye with much emotion, but Fr. Titus encouraged him from afar, "Everything will be fine."

We know about the last days of Fr. Titus thanks to a truly exceptional witness: his own executioner. Indeed, in her impressive testimony years later, *Tizia*, the nurse who gave the final injection to the elderly Carmelite, would recount everything that happened. Fearful of possible reprisals, she herself suggested the generic fake name of *Tizia*. Her testimony is still under the seal of secrecy in the General Postulation of the Carmelites in Rome. She would also confess that she never saw any of the prisoners leave alive who came to the infirmary already dying. Even before entering, many had already had their death report drawn up, a common form that was later sent to relatives, indicating that the prisoner had died of intestinal infection.

The figure of *Tizia* remains somewhat enigmatic, since she herself threw up a smokescreen over her identity. Apparently she was terrified of being considered a war criminal and had already been in a German jail for several years when she testified in the process. It seems that she was a young Dutch woman who at the age of 16 had moved to Berlin. There she had come into contact with both the structure and the mentality of the Reich. She was attracted by the force of its ideology, by the exalted values of the race which would annihilate everything that weakened it (particularly Jews, Communists, and Catholics). *Tizia* saw Hitler as a demigod who had replaced the old superstitions that Christianity had propagated for centuries. When the war began, she was sent to Dachau, in southern Germany, where hundreds of the dying passed through her hands and whom she helped to eliminate. *Tizia* told how she had become familiar with that job, like so many other nurses. They worked under the orders of Dr. Wolter—an enigmatic character, cold, calculating, totally inhuman—who was in charge of carrying out the experiments with the prisoners. Many photographs of them remain in the Dachau archives. Wolter carried out, for example, a large-scale experiment to analyze the results of different therapies for tuberculosis patients who had been selected from various camps. We know that during the years 1941 and 1942, Wolter had experimented on some clergymen who were in the camp, producing abscesses that were later treated in various ways. Dr. Wolter and his medical team regularly sent the information gathered from the experiments to the highest levels of the Reich. With certainty we know that one of the human beings who was used as a laboratory guinea pig was Fr. Titus Brandsma. Once, in his heartlessness, Wolter commented about Father Titus, "This man is really funny. He doesn't resist anything."

When he was admitted, Fr. Titus was very sick and weakened by the beatings and the camp's miserable living conditions. He had already been worn down by life in Scheveningen, Amersfoort, and Kleve. A few days before, he had been beaten by one of the *Kapos* and left abandoned in the mud for several hours. That had finished off his meager strength. In addition, he became the subject of several experiments. According to *Tizia*, he was perfectly aware of them. On one occasion he exclaimed, "Your will be done, Lord and not mine," which greatly impressed the young nurse. During the first days, Fr. Titus was still conscious and lucid; he spoke to the other sick people, encouraging them. This was his little apostolate there. On one occasion *Tizia* heard him chatting with another patient who slept in the same bunk. He said, "But if that is nothing, you will see how everything works out." He was an irrepressible optimist, even in the midst of a situation which totally invited despair.

Thanks to the tireless efforts of Brother Raphael with the German priests and with Fritz Kühr, a Catholic nurse who enjoyed a certain position in the camp, on certain occasions Fr. Titus was able to receive communion in the infirmary, clandestinely of course. This same nurse brought news of Fr. Titus to the group of "the Dutch" in their barracks, who were very concerned about the uncertain future of Fr. Titus. According to Brother Raphael, he would have received a visit from Hilary Januszewski, the young Carmelite prior of the Krakow community. He would have brought him communion. By sheer coincidence, it is also quite likely that he met the Luxembourg priest, Jean Bernard, in the infirmary. Bernard says that he left the infirmary on July 23, 1942.

Apparently, Fr. Titus occasionally spoke with *Tizia*, especially after he learned that she was of Dutch origin. *Tizia* recounts how the Carmelite impressed her from the first moment. She felt bad in his presence but, at the same time, she appreciated those kind gestures he showed her. On one occasion Fr. Titus gave her his rosary made with buttons, small splinters, and pieces of wood. *Tizia* told him that she neither knew how to pray, nor did she believe in it. Fr. Titus, undeterred and with great compassion, told her to at least repeat the second part of the Hail Mary, *Pray for us sinners*, and to ask for peace. Disarmed, she put that poor rosary in the pocket of her camp uniform. Without knowing it, she was preserving a whole relic. On another occasion *Tizia* told him that she despised priests, to which Fr. Titus responded by freely quoting Saint Teresa: "Good priests are not those who say beautiful words in the pulpits, but those who are capable of offering their pain for their fellow men. For this reason, I am happy to be able to suffer." *Tizia* could not understand that philosophy very well; it was so contrary to the concept of the *Übermensch* that the party had taught her.

Fr. Titus was gradually surrendering to the bed of pain. The prisoners outside knew that he barely ate and hardly ever got out of bed. In the long hours of waiting, perhaps the words of Saint Boniface, for whom Fr. Titus felt so much devotion and sympathy and whose devotion he had spread in his native Friesland and throughout the Netherlands, might have passed through his mind:

> Let us stand firm in the fight on the day of the Lord, for days of trouble and distress have come upon us. Let us die, if God so wishes, by the holy laws of our fathers, so that we deserve, like them, to obtain the eternal inheritance.

July 26 was a Sunday. In the morning Dr. Wolter made a routine visit, keeping his distance from the sick. On these visits someone was always singled out for the fatal injection. On that day only Fr. Titus was chosen. At 1:30 p.m. Wolter gave the order mechanically, and without paying too much attention, stamped his signature on one more form. At 2:00 p.m. *Tizia* began to prepare the injection, a carbolic acid compound, whose effects would be very quick. By 2:10 p.m. Fr. Titus was dead. His body, like so many others, was lost to the anonymity of the crematoria that daily vomited a brown smoke with that sickly sweet smell.

That same afternoon, Brother Raphael met with one of the nurses who showed him Anno Sjoerd Brandsma's death report while laughing out loud. The group of Dutch prisoners was deeply saddened. "Uncle Titus" had died. Perhaps he would no longer suffer. *Tizia* left the infirmary. She had finished her shift for the day. It did not feel good. She was nervous and irritable. Something was wrong and she did not know what. An ideology demands that you believe at face value. You cannot doubt. You cannot interpret anything. You cannot enter the slightest crisis. If a single crack were to open up, it would end by shattering the entire rock. She left the camp for the small hotel where she kept her personal effects, and where she lived when there were no guards in the camp. She rummaged through her bag for a cigarette but pulled out a strange object. It was that grotesque rosary. She remembered the words of Fr. Titus. Perhaps we should ask for peace. A crack had appeared in the rock.

By one of those great coincidences in history, on the same Sunday when Fr. Titus was killed in Dachau, a letter from the bishops was read in all the churches of the Netherlands in which, with a considerably severe tone, the latest government regulations were criticized. The letter had been written in great secrecy and was only made public on Sunday the 26th. The audacity of the Dutch episcopate, one of the strongest in condemning National Socialism, caught the occupation government by surprise. The retaliation was harsh and included the arrest of vowed religious of Jewish origin. Because of this, Sister Teresa Benedicta of the Cross, Edith Stein, was arrested. A few days later she would die together with her sister in the hell of Auschwitz, after passing through the *Durchgangslager* in Amersfoort.

In Dachau the death of Fr. Titus was greeted with great regret. Although he had only been there for barely a month, his friendly character, pastoral and priestly concern, and his signs of holiness had left a deep impression on everyone.

A sketch of Fr. Titus Brandsma done by fellow Carmelite Br. Raphael Tijhuis during their internment together at the Dachau concentration camp. Brother Raphael survived the war.

Ut luceat omnibus

On August 5, 1942, an official notification came to Fr. Titus's brother-in-law, the husband of his sister Gatsche, informing him of the death of Anno Sjoerd Brandsma as a result of an intestinal infection. It noted as well that the corpse had been cremated. A series of official stamps, illegible signatures, and the steamroller of the system officially closed yet another case. The war continued its inexorable pace, leaving in its wake endless misery and a list of the innumerable dead and missing. On August 6, as soon as the news was received, Archbishop De Jong sent a note of condolence to the relatives of Fr. Titus. Perhaps, in a way, the prelate felt responsible for the death of the Carmelite, although the latter had already sent him a word of encouragement and absolute loyalty through various channels from the various prisons, as we saw above. That note to the family, from a man who a few years later would be elevated to the rank of cardinal, is significant:

> He was a religious saint and a holy priest, a man of great merit in many fields, an initiator of many works, always ready to help me, to whom I owe deep appreciation.

On August 11, 1942, only 16 days after the death of Fr. Titus, Fr. Hubert Driessen, a great friend of Titus' and his brother in Carmel—the same one who shortly before his arrest had advised him to be careful—wrote from the Merkelbeek monastery to another Carmelite who had also suffered the persecution of fascism, informing him of the death of his old friend. He wrote to Fr. Bartolomé Xiberta, a great theologian, who in 1937 had been expelled from Italy by the Mussolini government and who remained in Oss during his two years of exile. He knew well, therefore, the Dutch Carmelites and Fr. Titus in particular. Fr. Xiberta was then in the convent of Olot (Gerona). There he received the letter in which Driessen lamented the death of Fr. Titus and the prohibition of the occupation government against public funerals. He also commented on how this man's reputation for holiness had immediately spread among the nuns and Protestants.

On September 23 of the same year an academic memorial took place at the Catholic University of Nijmegen in which the Rector, Jacques van Hinneken, gave a very moderate gloss, without mentioning conflictive and dangerous issues, on some of the virtues of the former Rector of that University ten years before.

On April 30, 1945, the Allied troops took Munich and a few hours later entered Dachau. The liberation of the camp in which there had been, among the many thousands of prisoners, more than two thousand priests and religious, was a moving and terrible moment at the same time. It was an unforgettable sight: corpses piled up, hungry prisoners fiercely throwing themselves at the food that the soldiers had brought, abandoned sick people, the undead. The world was going to know Dachau and the other camps— not only to the shame of a single nation or age, but to the shame of all humanity that had been capable of creating such horrors.

A year later Spectrum, the publishing house with which Fr. Titus had been engaged, published his life of Saint Teresa despite the uncompleted manuscript. The edition was prepared by B. Meijer, who would become the first biographer of Fr. Titus. Professor Brandsma's approach to St. Teresa's story made a great impression on Dutch readers, who noted both the erudition and the iron willpower that Fr. Titus demonstrated in even the hardest moments, when everything invited discouragement.

On November 4, 1946, Queen Wilhelmina of the Netherlands wrote a note of condolence to the relatives of Fr. Titus, highlighting the value and example of his life, as both a religious and a civil figure. Also in 1946, after being tried in Nuremberg, Arthur Seyss-Inquart, Hitler's high commissioner for the Netherlands, was executed. While awaiting that execution by hanging, he returned to his lost faith and received communion after confessing to the prison chaplain.

In September 1954 a gathering of surviving interned priests took place at Dachau at which the suggested beatification of Fr. Titus was enthusiastically received.

On January 11, 1955, the beatification process began at the diocesan level. Little by little the support of bishops from all over the world began to arrive. So also arrived the witness of fellow prisoners and a little later, the direct testimony that would be decisive, unique, and overwhelming. The nurse *Tizia* openly told everything that had happened. She had returned to the Catholic faith of her parents that she had abandoned as a childhood memory for many years. *Tizia* was convinced that Father Titus, his intercession, or his example, had brought about her conversion to the faith.

On December 20, 1957, the process reached Rome, and just six years later the Cause entered the Congregation for the Cause of Saints.

In 1963, Pope John XXIII, the "good Pope," read a biography of Fr. Titus and pointed out that he had been so moved that it had even cost him a few sleepless nights.

On November 3, 1985, Fr. Titus Brandsma was beatified by John Paul II during a ceremony in Rome. The events began with a torchlight procession organized by German and Dutch youth, a symbol of reconciliation and peace. The prophetic words of Fr. Titus in his letter to Sergeant Hardegen had been fulfilled:

> God save the Netherlands! God save Germany! May God grant these two peoples to walk again in peace and freedom and recognize his Glory for the good of these two nations so close.

In 1992 in his homeland, the Archives of Catholic Friesland, organized an exhibition on Blessed Titus Brandsma, this noble son of the earth. It happened on the occasion of the 50th anniversary of his death. From this came the idea of creating a permanent museum and an archive on the figure of Titus Brandsma. The museum opened its doors in 2003 and was officially dedicated in January 2004. Since then, it has been promoting an awareness of Fr. Titus through a range of permanent and temporary exhibitions.

The tapestry that hung in St. Peter's Basilica during the beatification has been temporarily donated by the Postulator General of the Carmelites, Fr. Giovanni Grosso, to the Church of Saint Francis in Bolsward—a tribute to Titus' hometown and to the parish where his faith was received and nurtured during the first years of his life.

In 2007, the Dutch Bishops wrote to the Vatican to encourage the canonization of Brandsma. Cardinal Simonis signed the letter addressed to Cardinal Monsignor Saraiva Martins, Prefect of the Sacred Congregation for the Causes of Saints, on behalf of the Dutch Episcopal Conference of which Simonis was President. They advocated for progress in the cause of Titus and highlighted the positive impact that his canonization would have on the Dutch Church and society.

On October 1, 2010, the Titus Brandsma Memorial was inaugurated in the city of Nijmegen. Many Carmelite communities around the world participated in its creation, and their names appear on the bricks that make up the memorial. In the center stands a beautiful monument by the Dutch artist Arie Trum, who wanted to reflect the openness of Saint Titus, his spirit of dialogue, his devotion to Saint Teresa, and the firmness of his principles.

In August 2018, as part of a formation course for Carmelite students from around the world, the prior general of the Order dedicated a plaque at the Dachau Memorial in honor of the Carmelites who were interned there, several of whom died in the camp. The director of the memorial, Dr. Gabriele Hammermann, and the prioress of the enclosed Carmelite convent, *Karmel Heilig Blut*, welcomed the participants of the formation course. After the simple ceremony, during which the plaque was unveiled, a Eucharist was celebrated in the monastery chapel.

In recent years, two provinces of the Carmelite Order have adopted Titus as their protector and bear his name. Both cases are significant. The first was the new united province of Germany, fruit of the union of the two previously existing provinces. The new province was erected in 2012 and assumed the name of the Province of Blessed Titus Brandsma (now Province of St. Titus Brandsma). The other province is the Philippines, erected as a province in 2013. The mission in the Philippines was created in the 1970s by the Dutch Carmelites. In a way, it can be considered an extension of the Dutch Province's missionary spirit throughout the 20th century, which has borne such bountiful fruits as Indonesia and Brazil. As noted, the young Fr. Titus wanted to go to the missions in Java, but was not allowed by his superiors.

On November 26, 2020, the Medical Consultation, appointed by the Vatican Congregation for the Causes of Saints, recognized the impossibility of scientifically explaining the healing from advanced skin cancer of a North American Carmelite, Fr. Michael Driscoll. The cure was attributed to the intercession of Titus Brandsma.

Chronology of Titus Brandsma's Life

1881 - February 23: Anno Sjoerd Brandsma is born to Titus and Tjitje (née Postma) at a settlement made up of a handful of farmers known as Oegeklooster, near Bolsward in eastern Frisland. His father is a successful farmer. The Brandsmas will have six children, four daughters and two sons. While one daughter will marry, the other children will become religious.

1892-1898: Anno attends the Franciscan school in Megen, in the province of North Brabant. While studying there, his vocation to religious life matures. It is thought he will enter the Franciscan Order, but his fragile health denies him that possibility.

1898 - September 22: Anno enters the Carmelite noviтiate in Boxmeer. He takes the religious name of Titus, the same name as his father.

1899 - October 3: Titus Brandsma professes his first vows as a Carmelite.

1900-1905: Titus continues his studies in philosophy and theology at the Carmelite houses in Boxmeer, Zenderen, and Oss.

1901: Titus publishes his first book: a translation from the French of an anthology of the writings of the Spanish Carmelite mystic, St. Teresa of Jesus. His work is titled

Bloemlezing uit de werken der H. Teresia (Anthology of the Works of St. Teresa).

1905 - June 17: At 24 years of age, Titus Brandsma is ordained a priest in the cathedral of Den Bosch in Brabant.

1906-1909: Brandsma is sent to the international student house in Rome, Italy. He attends the philosophy program at the Gregorian Pontifical University and takes sociology classes at the *Istituto Leoniano*. He also begins writing for some Dutch newspapers and magazines.

During his summer vacations Titus travels to Mainburg in Bavaria, Germany. During one summer break, he has a reoccurrence of his stomach illness and is sent to the Carmelite house in Albano, near Rome, to recover.

1909 - October 25: Titus passes the doctoral exam in philosophy with the grade of *probatus*. He returns to the Netherlands the next day.

1909-1923: Brandsma begins his teaching career with the Carmelite students in Oss. He is assigned classes in philosophy, mathematics as well as other subjects. He is also named Regent of Studies.

1912: Brandsma starts a magazine about Carmelite culture called *Karmelrozen* (Rose of Carmel) which later is renamed *Speling*. After two years it has more than 13,000 subscribers.

1918: With a team of collaborators, Brandsma begins the translation (from the Spanish) and publication of a planned seven additional volumes of the works of St. Teresa in the Dutch language.

1919-1923: Titus is named editor-in-chief of the dying newspaper *De Stad Oss* (The City of Oss). It revives.

1923-1942: Brandsma becomes a professor at the newly founded Catholic University of Nijmegen. He teaches philosophy, the history of philosophy, and the history of Dutch mysticism.

1929: Brandsma travels in Spain where he gains a deep appreciation for the country's gentleness and culture and Carmelite heritage.

1932-1933: Brandsma is elected *rector magnificus* of the Catholic University of Nijmegen, a one-year position. To celebrate the opening of the school year, Brandsma gives his celebrated speech on the concept of God (*Godsbegrip*); he completes an official trip to Milan and Rome as *rector magnificus*.

1933: The elections in Germany are won by the National Socialist Party, and Adolf Hitler becomes chancellor.

1935: The Archbishop of Utrecht, Johannes De Jong, names Brandsma as the ecclesiastical assistant to the Association of Catholic Journalist (*R. K. Journalistenvereniging*), a group of approximately 30 publications. He obtains his international journalist card.

Brandsma travels to Ireland and the United States where he gives conferences on Carmelite spirituality and tradition, subsequently collected in the book *The Beauty of Carmel* (*La bellezza del Carmelo*).

1938-1939: Titus gives lectures on the National Socialist (Nazi) ideology, criticizing its pagan and anti-human approach.

1940 - May 10: The German army invades the Netherlands, Belgium, Luxembourg, and France, gradually imposing its own ideology.

1941 - January 26: The Dutch Church, through their bishops, reacts firmly. Fr. Titus actively collaborates with them. Moreover, he was entrusted with the presidency of the Association of Catholic Schools.

1941 - December 30: Archbishop De Jong summons Fr. Titus for a discussion about the difficult situation of the Catholic press.

1942 - Early January: During the first days of January,

Brandsma visits the editorial offices of the Catholic newspapers to deliver the directives of the bishops and to encourage the editors to resist Nazi pressure to publish their propaganda.

1942 - January 19: Upon returning from the university, Fr. Titus is arrested at the Carmelite monastery in Nijmegen. He passes his first night in the Arnhem jail.

1942 - January 20-March 12: Brandsma is taken to Scheveningen prison where he is interrogated. He strongly reaffirms his anti-Nazi positions. The official in charge of the questioning, a secularized priest, did not destroy the notes from the interrogation. They become part of the beatification process.

Titus is allowed to keep two books with him: *The Life of St. Teresa of Jesus* translated by Thomas Kwakman and *The Life of Jesus* by Cyril Verschaeve. During this time, he decides to write the life of St. Teresa, a project conceived many years before but never brought to fruition. In the absence of paper, he continues writing his manuscript between the lines of the book *The Life of Jesus*.

1942 - March 12-April 28: Brandsma is transferred to the "transit" camp of Amersfoort. He is forced to work and live in very difficult conditions. On Good Friday he delivers a conference on Geert Groote, an important figure in Dutch spirituality.

1942 - April 28-May 16: Fr. Titus returns again to the Scheveningen prison camp for a follow-up interrogation.

1942 - May 16-June 13: Brandsma is relocated to the Kleve "transit" camp. He finds some relief from the suffering endured at Amersfoort. At Kleve he is allowed to participate in Mass and have spiritual talks with the chaplain of the camp. In the meantime, his religious superiors try, in vain, to change his sentence to house arrest so he is permitted to live in a German religious house.

1942 - June 13-19: Brandsma is transported with other prisoners by train in an animal car via Cologne, Frankfurt, and Nüremberg, to the infamous Dachau concentration camp.

The Dachau internment camp had been constructed at the beginning of the 1930s, initially for political prisoners. During the war, the camp holds at least 110,000 people, of which only 30,000 survived. Inhumane experiments are performed on some prisoners, especially those who are disabled or too weak to be productive in the forced work details.

1942 - June 19-July18: Brandsma is housed in Block 28, set aside for religious and priests. He meets his fellow Dutch Carmelite Raphael Tijhuis, a brother from the community in Mainz, Germany. Brother Raphael is imprisoned because he complained about the difficulty of finding stamps in a letter to his family. Brother Raphael becomes Brandsma's companion in his final days. He will be a principal witness at Brandsma's beatification process.

1942 - July 18-26: Fr. Titus is kept in the prison hospital. A nurse gives him a lethal injection of carbolic acid at 2 pm on Sunday, July 26. A short time before his death, he gives that nurse a rosary made by a fellow prisoner. The woman later converts to the Catholic faith and testifies in Brandsma's beatification process.

1955: The diocesan process for the beatification and canonization of Brandsma is initiated in the Diocese of Den Bosch, in the Netherlands.

1971: The first examination of the letters by the Congregation of the Causes of the Saints takes place.

1973: The process for beatification is introduced a second time for procedural reasons.

1979: The Acts are presented to the Congregation for the Causes of the Saints.

1983: The cause is readmitted as a case for martyrdom.

1984: The theological consultors and the Congregation of Cardinals give positive opinions for Brandsma's martyrdom. Pope John Paul II signs the decree on martyrdom.

1985 - November 5: Pope John Paul II solemnly proclaims Carmelite Titus Brandsma as a blessed and as a martyr of the faith.

1992: In Brandsma's native Frisland, an Archive of Catholic Frisia is created on the occasion of the 50th anniversary of the death of Blessed Titus. A presentation on this noble son is organized and the idea of creating a permanent museum and archive on the life of Titus Brandsma takes hold. The museum opens its doors in 2003 and is officially inaugurated in January 2004. Over time, the story of Fr. Titus is promoted, and various presentations and temporary exhibits are organized at the museum.

The tapestry from the beatification is temporarily loaned to the church of St. Francis in Bolsward by the Postulator General of the Carmelites, Fr. Giovanni Groso, as a homage to his birth city and to the parish where he received and nourished his faith during the first years of his life.

2005: Titus Brandsma is chosen by the citizens of the town as *Nijmegen's Greatest Citizen of All Time*.

2007: Cardinal Simonis, as president of the Dutch Episcopal Conference, writes a letter on behalf of the other Dutch bishops to Cardinal Saraiva Martins, prefect of the Congregation for the Causes of the Saints, encouraging the canonization of Blessed Titus Brandsma. The letter highlights the very positive effect that his canonization would have on the Dutch Church and Dutch society.

2010 - October 1: The Titus Brandsma Memorial is inaugurated in the City of Nijmegen. Participating are many Carmelite communities from around the world and their names appear on the bricks which create the memorial.

In the center is a beautiful monument constructed by the Dutch artist Arie Trum. He wished the artwork to reflect the openness of St. Titus, his skill at dialogue, his devotion to St. Teresa, and the strength of his principles.

2012-2013: In recent years, two provinces of the Carmelite Order adopt Titus as protector and take his name. The first is the newly united province of Germany, fruit of the union of the long-established Upper German Province and the Lower German Province which Titus Brandsma played a role in re-establishing after the Secularization. The new province was erected in 2012 and assumed the name "The Province of Blessed Titus Brandsma." The other province is that of the Philippines, erected as province in 2013. The Carmelite foundation in the Philippines had been a mission created 70 years earlier by the Dutch Carmelite province.

2018 - August: While participating in a formation course for Carmelite students from various provinces around the world, the Prior General of the Order, Most Rev. Fernando Millán Romeral, unveils a plaque in the Memorial of Dachau to honor the Carmelites who were interned there, some of whom died in the camp. After the simple ceremony of unveiling the plaque, the group celebrates Eucharist in the chapel of the Heilig Blut Carmelite monastery.

2020 - November 26: The Medical Consultation, appointed by the Vatican Congregation of the Causes of the Saints, recognizes the impossibility of scientific explanation for the cure from cancer of the Carmelite, Fr. Michael Driscoll. The cure is attributed to the intercession of Blessed Titus Brandsma.

2021 - May 25: The Congress of Theological Consultors recognized the miracle attributed to the intercession of Blessed Titus Brandsma, O. Carm., relating to the scientifically inexplicable healing of Fr. Michael Driscoll, O.

Carm., from cancer.

2021 - November 25: During an audience given to Cardinal Marcello Semeraro, prefect of the Congregation for the Causes of the Saints, Pope Francis authorized the Congregation to promulgate the decrees regarding the miracle attibuted to the intercession of Blessed Titus Brandsma.

2022 - March 4: During an Ordinary Public Consistory held in the Vatican's Consistory Hall in the Apostolic Palace, Pope Francis announced May 15, 2022 as the date for the canonization of Blessed Titus Brandsma.

2022 - May 15: Pope Francis canonizes Titus Brandsma as a martyr for the faith. Nine other blesseds were also canonized during the same ceremony. Two Masses of Thanksgiving were held in the days immediately following. On Monday, May 16, a Mass was held at the Altar of the Chair in St. Peter's Basilica with Cardinal Willem Jacobus Eijk. The following evening Mass was celebrated at the Carmeltie church of Santa Maria in Traspontina.

BIBLIOGRAPHIC NOTES

Without any pretense of exhausting all of the available materials, we offer the following works to English-language readers who want to deepen their knowledge of the life and thought of Saint Titus.

A good bibliography current to the date of the beatification in 1985, prepared by Father Adrian Staring, can be found in Adrian Staring, "Bibliografia di Tito Brandsma" in *Carmelus* 31 (1984) 209-230.

Every year the journal *Carmelus* includes a section dedicated to Fr. Titus in its *Bibliographia Carmelitana Annualis*.

A project to make all of the existing speeches, articles, correspondence and other writings of Saint Titus available in English has resulted in the publication of seven volumes entitled *The Collected Works of Titus Brandsma*. The series is published by Edizioni Carmelitane in Rome.

There are several highly recommended biographies of St. Titus Brandsma in English:

Josse Alzin, *A Dangerous Little Friar* (Dublin 1957). [translation from the 1954 French original, *Ce petit moine dangereux*]

Miguel Arribas, *The Price of Truth: Titus Brandsma Carmelite* (Darien: Carmelite Media, 2021)

[translation from the 1998 Spanish original, *El precio de la verdad: Tito Brandsma Carmelita*]

Constant Dölle, *Encountering God In The Abyss* (Leuven-Paris 2002).

Joseph Rees, *Titus Brandsma* (London 1971).

In other languages, the most important ones:

The works by Aukes, Meijer and Vallainc, among others are the most significant.

H.W.F. Aukes, *Het Leven van Titus Brandsma* (Utrecht-Antwerpen 1961).

[There is an English translation-adaptation, done by Anthony Vanden Heuvel: AUKES, H.W.F., *Titus Brandsma: A Modern Martyr for the Truth* (Welland-Ontario 1996)]

Brocardus Meijer, *Titus Brandsma* (Bossum 1951).

Fausto Vallainc, *Un Giornalista martire* (Milano 1985).

On St. Titus's confrontation with Nazism, these works should be noted:

Leopold Glueckert, *Titus Brandsma: Friar Against Fascism* (Darien, Illinois, 1985) [republished 2004].

C. Bonetto, "Il giornalismo cattolico secondo Titus Brandsma." *Carmelus* 41 (1994) 126-164 [in Italian]

As for the fellow prisoners:

We will limit ourselves to the testimonies of two Carmelite brothers who lived with him in Dachau:

Albert Urbanski, *Duchowni w Dachau* (Krakow 1945) [in Polish]

Raphael Tijhuis, *Nothing Can Stop God from Reaching Us* (Rome 2007).

On Hilarius Januszewski:

For information on fellow Carmelite Dachau inmate also beatified by St. Pope John Paul II, see the letter of the former prior general, Fr. Joseph Chalmers, titled: *Hilarius Januszewski, Carmelite: Faithful in Little, Faithful in Much*. It was published, among other places, in *Carmel in the World* 37 (1999/3) 165-174.

Regarding some specific aspects of Brandsma's spirituality:

It is worth highlighting, above all, the very complete collection of various studies on his biography and his spiritual profile, accompanied by a selection of texts by Fr. Titus that was published (in English) on the occasion of his beatification. Works on his biography, his spiritual dimension, his mystical experience, joy, devotion to Saint Teresa, simplicity of life, etc., are included:

AA.VV., *Essays on Titus Brandsma* (Rome 1985) [there is a 2004 reprint].

Among many other articles and works, we can mention:

Hein Blommestijn, "In His Image: Blessed Titus Brandsma." *The Canadian Catholic Review* 4 (1986) 139-145.

A. Breij, "The Spiritual Life of Titus Brandsma." *The Sword* 22 (1962) 148-158.

Eammon Carroll, "Blessed Titus Brandsma, Carmelite Scholar of Our Lady." *Our Lady's Digest* 40 (1986) 105-107.

B. Hanley, *No Strangers to Violence, No Strangers to Love*. (Notre Dame-Indiana, 1983) 176-201.

_____, "Blessed Titus Brandsma." *Catholic Digest* (December 1985) 69-79.

Jos Huls-Hein H. Blommestijn, "Titus Brandsma's Mystagogical Approach to the Suffering of Christ," in Titus Brandsma, *Ecce Homo. Contemplating the Way of Love (Meditations on the Way of the Cross of Albert Servaes)* (Leuven 2003) 7-18.

Jane Lytle-Vieira, *Meditations with Titus Brandsma* (Darien, Illinois, 2004).

M. Malham, "Mystic in a Train Compartment," in *By Fire into Light. Four Catholic Martyrs of the Nazi Camps* (Leuven-Paris 2002) 7-68. [Fiery Arrow]

Wilfred McGreal, "An Open Letter to Titus Brandsma." *Mount Carmel* 46 (1998/2) 14-16.

Fernando Millán Romeral. "Seekers of the Living God in Dark Times." *The Sword* 70 (2010) 105-121.

_____, "Titus Brandsma: An Inspirational Figure for Lay Carmelites." *The Sword* 72 (2012) 69-82.

_____, "Blessed Titus Brandsma: Translator, Scholar and Devotee of St. Teresa." *The Sword* 73 (2013) 97-120.

_____, "Titus Brandsma and His International Promotion." *Carmel in the World* 56 (2017 \ 1) 6-12.

_____, "The Poem of Blessed Titus Brandsma in English, Esperanto and Interlingua." *The Sword* 78 (2018) 69-96.

_____, "Titus Brandsma: A Carmelite Pioneer of Ecumenism," in AA.VV., *Revisiting the Fountain of Elijah* [K. Alban - J. Bergström Allen, eds.] (Rome 2018) 67-81.

_____, "Titus Brandsma a Man of Openness and Dialogue." *Carmel in the World* 58 (2019 \ 2) 111-117.

B.J. Nolan, "Becoming God-Bearers: the Marian Devotion of Titus Brandsma" *Mount Carmel* 57 (4/2009) 44-50.

Steven Payne, *Spirituality in History* (Liturgical Press, Collegeville 2011) 135-146.

K. Tamura, Blessed Titus Brandsma O. Carm. "A Reflection of the 50th Anniversary of His Martyrdom." *Carmel in the World* 33 (1994-1) 31-41.

Leander Troy, "Blessed Titus Brandsma's Trip to the United States and Canada in 1935." *The Sword* 52 (1992) 25-35.

Redemptus Valabek, "Blessed Titus Brandsma and Our Lady," in *Carmel and Mary* [J.F. Welch, ed.] (Washington 2002) 89-105.

_____, "Mary and Ourselves: God Bearers." *Carmel in the World* 18 (1979) 203-227.

_____, "Prayer and Contemplation in the Life of Blessed Titus Brandsma," in *Profiles in Holiness IV* (Rome 2011) 79-91.

A veritable arsenal of data and texts of Fr. Titus translated into Italian can be found in the minutes of the beatification process:

Summarium super dubio beatificationis seu declarationis martyrii servi dei Titi Brandsma (Buscoducen) (Rome 1979).

Regarding the works of Titus Brandsma himself, we highlight:

The lectures he gave in English in the United States and Canada in 1935 have been published multiple times. The text of which was prepared by Leo Walter, O. Carm. and first published under the title *Carmelite Mysticism. Historical Sketches* (Chicago 1936), and later as *The Beauty of Carmel* (Dublin-London 1955); and in small booklets, under the title *Carmelite Mysticism* (Faversham 1980). There is also a tribute edition on the 50th anniversary of these conferences: *Carmelite Mysticism. Historical Sketches* (Darien, Illinois 1986 and reissued in 2004).

Regarding some of his articles and works translated into English, we highlight:

Titus Brandsma, "The True Devotion to Mary" (Discourse delivered at the Marian Congress held in Zenderen, August 15-18, 1931). *Carmel in the World* 32 (1993-2) 76-82

_____, "The Heart of the Mystical Life: St John of the Cross and Mary's Motherhood of God." *Carmel in the World* 32 (1993/2) 116-122.

_____, "Peace and Love for Peace." *Carmel in the World* 33 (1994-1) 4-16. [Translated by P. J. Smet]

_____, *In Search of Living Water. Essays on the Mystical Heritage of the Netherlands* (Leuven 2013).

_____, *Meditations on the Way of the Cross of Albert Servaes* (Darien-Illinois, 2004).

_____, *Ecce homo. Contemplating the Way of Love (Meditations on the Way of the Cross of Albert Servaes)* (Leuven, 2003).

RECOMMENDED CARMELITE WEBSITES

For more information about the Carmelites today,
our spirituality and our ministries worldwide, visit:

The Carmelite Order: ocarm.org

The Most Pure Heart of Mary Province: carmelites.net

Center for Carmelite Studies at Catholic University of America:
carmelites.info/CenterForCarmeliteStudies

Carmelite Institute of North America:
carmeliteinstitute.net

For a listing of Carmelite provinces worldwide, visit:
carmelites.info/provinces

For a listing of Monasteries of Carmelite nuns, visit:
carmelites.info/nuns

For a listing of Carmelite Hermitages, please visit:
carmelites.info/hermits

For a listing of sites about Lay Carmelites:
carmelites.info/lay carmel

For a listing of Affiliated Congregations and Institutes:
carmelites.info/congregations

For our work with the United Nations, visit:
carmelitengo.org

For more information about publications, visit:
carmelites.info/publications

www.ingramcontent.com/pod-product-compliance
Lightning Source LLC
Chambersburg PA
CBHW060135100426
42744CB00007B/793